Bitcoin

Mastering And Profiting From Bitcoin Cryptocurrency Using

Mining, Trading And Investing Techniques

By David Spencer

If you like my book, please leave a positive review on Amazon. I would appreciate it a lot. Thanks! This is the link:

Leave your review here. Thank you!

Contents

In this guide, you will be taught all about Bitcoin (BTC) and cryptocurrency, how they work, why they exist and what sort of innovation is behind Bitcoin. It wasn't too long prior when individuals began hearing the words 'Bitcoin' and 'digital forms of money.'

Scarcely any individuals outside of the crypto-groups realized what they were and many idea it was simply one more craze that will undoubtedly bomb in a couple of years or something like that. The estimation of one bitcoin was only a couple of pennies then so clearly it wasn't justified regardless of a ton. Consequently, it was disregarded by the majority. There were significantly more beneficial speculations one could make, all things considered.

The individuals who contributed entireties of cash on the new advanced money either had confidence in the framework proposed by its organizer, Satoshi Nakamoto, or they basically needed to perceive how it functions.

In any case, the individuals who accepted were compensated incredibly, and keep on being remunerated, as a solitary bitcoin now costs a huge number of dollars.

It just took Bitcoin five years to break the $1,000 stamp in late 2013, and only a couple of years after the fact, Bitcoin costs are at an untouched high – path past the $10,000 check for a solitary bitcoin!

With soaring costs and to a great degree quick development, an ever increasing number of individuals are interested about bitcoins and digital currencies all in all.

A Look At Cryptocurrency and Bitcoin's Colorful Past

Cryptographic forms of money are computerized monetary standards which are electronic in nature. They don't have a physical frame like paper cash or coins which you presumably have in your wallet at the present time. You can't hold them physically, yet you can purchase things with them.

Contingent upon the trader you're working with, they may acknowledge more than one digital money as installment.

As per CoinMarketCap, there are more than 1,000 dynamic cryptographic forms of money at this moment. In case you're hoping to contribute your well deserved money yet can't bear the cost of Bitcoin costs at the present time, there are a lot of elective digital forms of money to browse, for example, Ethereum, Litecoin, Ripple, Dash, Monero, Zcash, and the sky is the limit from there.

We would, obviously, encourage you to destroy some profundity investigate on the digital currency you need to put resources into as not all cryptographic forms of money are equivalent. Some are more steady than others and would, along these lines, improve for ventures.

Bitcoin isn't the world's first digital money; however it is the best. Many have preceded it yet all have fizzled. Furthermore, the explanation behind disappointment? Virtual cash had a characteristic issue – it was anything but difficult to twofold spend.

You could pay $100 to one shipper and utilize a similar measure of cash to pay a moment vendor! Con artists and fraudsters basically adored this escape clause.

Luckily, in 2007, Satoshi Nakamoto began dealing with the Bitcoin idea. On October 31st the next year, he discharged his white paper entitled "Bitcoin: A Peer-to-Peer Electronic Cash System" which plot an installment framework that tended to the twofold spending issue of computerized monetary forms.

It was a splendid idea that drew the consideration of the cryptographic group. The Bitcoin Project programming was enlisted in SourceForge only barely seven days after the white paper was distributed.

In January 2009, the primary ever Bitcoin piece called the 'Beginning square' was mined. Days after the fact, piece 170 recorded the main ever bitcoin exchange between Hal Finney and Satoshi Nakamoto.

The exact one year from now, in November 2010, Bitcoin's market top surpassed $1,000,000! This was an exceptionally significant minute in the advancement of Bitcoin as this prompt more individuals getting intrigued and putting resources into bitcoins. The cost now was $0.50/BTC.

In any case, in June 2011, Bitcoin encountered the alleged "Incredible Bubble of 2011" subsequent to achieving an unsurpassed high of $31.91/BTC. Only 4 days in the wake of achieving its most elevated value, the conversion scale plunged to simply $10/BTC.

Numerous financial specialists froze at losing so much cash and sold at a misfortune. It took just about 2 years for the swapping scale to recuperate and outperform the past unequaled high. The individuals who kept their bitcoins settled on the correct choice as the cost has kept on climbing and outperform everybody's desires.

What's extremely fascinating about Bitcoin is that while all exchanges are open and nothing is avoided anybody, nobody really knows anything about Satoshi Nakamoto.

Many have hypothesized that he isn't only one individual but instead an aggregate nom de plume a gathering of cryptographic engineers. Some have approached guaranteeing to be Satoshi, yet to date, his genuine personality remains a mystery.

For What Reason Do Cryptocurrencies Exist?

Many individuals have begun feeling that digital forms of money, Bitcoin specifically, are on the very edge of supplanting our national monetary standards, for example, the US Dollar, British Pound Sterling, Euro, Canadian Dollars, and that's only the tip of the iceberg. This is on account of digital currencies have begun to end up plainly exceptionally feasible other options to customary money.

Digital forms of money exist to address shortcomings in customary monetary forms which are, obviously, supported by national banks and governments. This makes conventional monetary standards inclined to defilement and control, among a large group of different issues.

Not at all like customary monetary forms, there is no overseeing body that backs Bitcoin and different digital currencies which implies they aren't subjected to anyone's impulses.

Bitcoin is totally decentralized, open source and straightforward. This implies you can see every one of the exchanges that have ever been done on the system and you can check and audit the blockchain information yourself to confirm the validness of every exchange.

Bitcoin keeps running on exceptionally complex numerical calculations to manage the production of new bitcoins and to ensure no twofold spending ever happens on the system (recollect, this is the Achilles' foot sole area of fizzled virtual monetary standards previously Bitcoin).

The Bitcoin code is so secure and propelled that it's for all intents and purposes difficult to cheat the framework so in case you're supposing you can make a boundless number of bitcoins, you're extraordinarily mixed up.

One of the fundamental issues of customary money is that these aren't constrained in number. This implies governments and national banks can print more cash when they see fit.

At the point when more cash is printed and enters the economy, this lessens the buying influence of our paper cash which implies we have to spend more for a thing we've just spent a couple of dollars on earlier; this is called expansion.

Bitcoin, then again, is an alternate story. The Bitcoin Protocol expresses that lone 21,000,000 bitcoins can ever be mined and made which implies that bitcoin is, truth be told, a rare asset.

Additionally, similar to national monetary forms, bitcoins are detachable, much like pennies to a dollar. The littlest bitcoin unit is known as a Satoshi, and it is 1/100,000,000 of a bitcoin. This implies you can contribute a couple of thousand Satoshis at once until the point that you at long last get an entire bitcoin.

Obviously, on the off chance that you go this course, it might set aside you some opportunity to get to 1 BTC yet in the event that the value keeps on soaring, at that point purchasing a couple of Satoshis consistently may pay off in the long haul.

Another motivation behind why digital forms of money are picking up in notoriety is that it is exceptionally compact which implies you can carry it with you anyplace you go. You can do likewise with physical cash and gold. In any case, a vast sum will prompt a substantial load on your wallet or pack.

Take a stab at putting a million dollars in an attaché or conveying a pack of gold! It's absolutely not as light as it looks in motion pictures.

With digital currency, you have distinctive wallet decisions, which are all exceptionally versatile, so you can without much of a stretch make installments at whatever point and wherever you need.

Bitcoins are not subject to bank and government directions. This implies you don't have to pay those strong bank charges which you cause at whatever point you send installments to other individuals.

You likewise don't have to hold up a few hours or possibly a couple of days for your installments to clear or post as bitcoin installments are made in a split second (more often than not in 10-45 minutes).

How Bitcoin Works

In this area, we will do our best to clarify the Bitcoin procedure as just as conceivable without going into an excessive amount of specialized language.

The principal thing you have to do is get yourself some bitcoins. You can either mine this yourself, get some as installment for products or administrations, or purchase at a Bitcoin trade like Coinbase or Kraken. There are distinctive wallets for you to store your new bitcoins in.

You can utilize a work area wallet, versatile application wallet, paper wallet, equipment wallet or an online wallet. There are upsides and downsides to each sort of wallet.

Nonetheless, most specialists concur that online wallets, particularly those on trade destinations, are not all that safe in light of the fact that both your private and open keys are spared on the web. This makes your wallet exceedingly defenseless against programmers.

When you've chosen the most reasonable wallet for your requirements, you would then be able to begin making bitcoin exchanges. To send bitcoin to another client, you should simply get their email or bitcoin address, enter the sum you wish to send, compose a snappy note to reveal to them what the installment is for (this is discretionary), and hit the Send catch!

On the other hand, in the event that you have the QR code to their bitcoin wallet, you can just output it and hit Send. The exchange will show up in the other individual's record in a brief timeframe, for the most part between 10-45 minutes. The explanation behind this 'pause' is clarified all the more completely in the following segment.

What's more, that is it! Bitcoin exchanges are snappy, protected, shabby and the ideal other option to paying with bank-issued credit and charge cards, and notwithstanding paying in real money.

The Technology Behind Bitcoin

At first glance, Bitcoin exchanges seem, by all accounts, to be quick and simple – and they genuinely are. Notwithstanding, off camera, the innovation that makes the Bitcoin arrange run consistently is a huge record known as the blockchain.

It's enormous on the grounds that it contains a record of all bitcoin exchanges that have ever occurred since Bitcoin was first discharged in 2009.

As additional time goes by and more exchanges happen, the measure of the blockchain will keep on growing. So here is the means by which the blockchain works:

When you send an installment, your wallet or application conveys a demand to the whole Bitcoin organize which is comprised of PCs or hubs. These hubs at that point approve your exchange utilizing known calculations.

Once your exchange is checked and affirmed, it is then joined with different exchanges to make another square of information for the blockchain.

This new square is then added to the finish of the blockchain. At the point when this happens, the exchange ends up plainly total and is presently changeless.

This whole procedure takes around 10-45 minutes all the way (this is the reason Bitcoin exchanges don't occur in a flash). Once the exchange is finished, nobody can fix or erase the exchange. The individual you've sent the bitcoin installment to (the beneficiary) will now observe your installment in his wallet.

So who checks and affirms exchanges if there's no focal body administering the system?

The appropriate response is the excavators. The mineworkers are truly the soul of the whole bitcoin organize. Some have even contrasted diggers with being hamsters in the wheel that keep the whole Bitcoin arrange going! Furthermore, this is valid.

Diggers assume such a gigantic part in the accomplishment of Bitcoin that they genuinely merit getting remunerated in valuable bitcoins. Without them, no new squares would be made and added to the blockchain.

On the off chance that nothing is added to the blockchain, no exchanges are ever finished. This implies no bitcoins installments are sent and got by anybody on the system. No new bitcoins will be made.

Since mineworkers are key to the Bitcoin arrange, they are made up for their diligent work as far as bitcoins (it would not bode well to remunerate them in conventional paper cash). They are relatively similar to workers of the system.

Since there are just a predetermined number of bitcoins (21 million), the quantity of bitcoins that mineworkers are paid with will keep on dwindling until all bitcoins are depleted by around 2140.

Since you realize what Bitcoin and digital money are about, we should go to the following aide where you will figure out how the estimation of bitcoin is resolved.

Chapter 1: Bitcoin Value – How Is The Value Of Bitcoin Determined

Bitcoin has been getting a tremendous measure of buildup as of late. It's one of the numerous advanced monetary standards in presence today which acts and capacities like customary cash however exists completely electronically—like information inside PCs.

What's more, that can be somewhat befuddling, in light of the fact that if there is no real physical bitcoin:

• How would it be able to have esteem?

• How would you be able to utilize digital money in a physical world?

Well really, the topic of how bitcoin has any esteem whatsoever isn't so far away from the topic of how most true cash has esteem.

For one thing, Bitcoin has no real inherent esteem, which implies that it has almost no utilization to us outside of its financial setting. However, the same can be said for most genuine monetary forms: cash just has esteem on the grounds that the legislature that issues it says it does.

This is called 'fiat cash,' since its esteem isn't attached to any physical ware and depends on the support of an administration.

However, not at all like fiat money, Bitcoin does not have an issuing expert that gives it esteem. Bitcoin is a decentralized money, which means there is no administering body that controls its creation and exchanges.

It doesn't reply to any legislature or association, so there isn't generally a motivation behind why it ought to have esteem, yet it does - and it would all be able to be come down to utility, shortage, and free market activity.

Bitcoin's Value Lies In Its Utility

Before we examine the utility of Bitcoin, first you should comprehend the nuts and bolts of how it functions. You are associated with the group of Bitcoin clients through a PC arrange, and the records that Bitcoin utilizes is known as a blockchain: exchanges are assembled into squares, which thusly are associated in a chain-like way, consequently the name.

The record managers are called mineworkers, since what they are doing, basically, sounds especially like gold excavators who strive to discover gold: they are working for the reward as bitcoins, which, similar to gold, are constrained in supply.

So now you know how Bitcoin functions. What does that need to do with its esteem? Everything, really. Bitcoin's esteem is in its utility: its decentralization, security, and simplicity of exchange.

To start with, we should take a gander at Bitcoin's decentralized framework. Bitcoin is outlined to such an extent that there is no requirement for any overseeing specialist to control it. It works through a distributed system where all exchanges are recorded in the blockchain.

On the most fundamental level, this would imply that it isn't attached to any state and accordingly is the main really borderless money. This means you can lead exchanges with individuals from various nations effectively in light of the fact that you're utilizing a similar money.

On a more profound, significantly more muddled level, the decentralization of Bitcoin's framework makes the likelihood of changing the back business.

The fund business offers various approaches to rearrange exchanges for simplicity of comfort. There are credit and charge cards, cash exchanging frameworks, electronic bank exchanges, and so forth. In any case, these frameworks need a go between to work—they require an organization or specialist to encourage the trade.

What's more, what you're doing at whatever point you make an exchange is that you're putting your trust on the mediator—that they will get your cash through or guard your cash in addition to other things. There is likewise the matter of exchange expenses, which, thought about per exchange, isn't excessively, however can without much of a stretch heap up after some time. What Bitcoin does is it disposes of the requirement for these brokers.

As said over, all exchanges in the Bitcoin arrange are recorded in the blockchain by mineworkers. While the blockchain and mineworker organize has the similarity of an administering body as in it monitors all bitcoins in presence, it's still in people in general space and hence can't be cornered.

This implies no single individual or gathering of people has a hang on the system—which, thusly, implies that bitcoins can remain completely straightforward and nonpartisan in its exchanges.

However, in the event that there is no official body going about as a controller, who would you be able to trust to ensure that exchanges do experience? The appropriate response: nobody. What's more, it sounds terrible, however it's really something to be thankful for.

The Bitcoin framework is intended to work without the requirement for trust. It's just plain obvious, it's not just an advanced cash, it's a cryptographic money, which implies that it is intensely in light of encryption systems to guard it.

Rather than working in view of client trust, Bitcoin works utilizing attempted and tried science (more on that later). Swindling the system is unimaginable because of its open condition.

That, as well as the framework is scrambled with the goal that attempting to submit extortion would require an amazingly expansive measure of registering power, which would by then have been more helpful on the off chance that you simply utilized it to mine more bitcoins.

The security framework, beside guaranteeing the unwavering quality of Bitcoin exchanges, likewise guarantees that the character of the Bitcoin clients can be ensured. Not at all like in Visas, your record number does not have any an incentive in your exchanges, which are eventually checked utilizing a private and open key.

It works this way: you put a computerized mark to your exchanges utilizing your private key which can be checked by the clients of the system utilizing your open key. The keys are encoded with the goal that the general population key can just ever work on the off chance that you had utilized the right private key in any case.

This implies:

1. Your personality can't be stolen by offenders to make false exchanges in your name.

2. You can remain totally mysterious in the Bitcoin arrange, which may demonstrate helpful for a few.

Ultimately, bitcoins have the likelihood of giving a simplicity of comfort that outperforms the conventional paying strategies that we as of now have now. As per the Bitcoin site, utilizing bitcoins permit you "to send and get bitcoins anyplace on the planet whenever.

No bank occasions. No fringes. No administration. Bitcoin enables its clients to be in full control of their cash."

Bitcoins Are Incredibly Scarce

Fiat cash has an in fact boundless supply as in governments can create cash at whatever point they need. Clearly, they don't do that since it will prompt swelling, so the creation and arrival of cash is controlled by the administration in view of escalated explore on advertise patterns and needs. Bitcoin, as you may have speculated, does not work the same.

Since Bitcoin is decentralized, there is no expert that chooses when to make new bitcoins. The framework is planned with the goal that new bitcoins must be made as a major aspect of a reward framework for the diggers.

Also, the reward is merited: the foundation of the Bitcoin framework is cryptography, or the craft of composing and understanding codes which requires a powerful measure of work to comprehend.

To refresh the blockchain, excavators from everywhere throughout the world need to race to take care of a particular math issue called SHA-256, which remains for Secure Hash Algorithm 256 piece.

It's fundamentally a math issue wherein you're given a yield and you should discover the information, such as settling for x and y given that $x + y = 2$.

The best way to take care of this sort of issue is through mystery, and to comprehend the SHA-256, you'd need to experience a crazy measure of conceivable arrangements previously you discover the appropriate response—for which you'd require a to a great degree effective (also costly) PC.

Mineworkers contribute a considerable measure of cash on these supercomputers (and additionally the immense measure of power it needs to run) all to mine new Bitcoins.

Jason Bloomberg, in an article for Forbes, composes that the estimation of Bitcoin is illustrative of this exertion: since mining bitcoins take diligent work, they turn out to be more valuable. So, first point to its shortage is that bitcoins are rare. You'd require a sizeable speculation just to have the capacity to make new bitcoins.

Yet, they're even made scarcer because of the way that there can just ever be a sure number of bitcoins in presence, which is 21 million. (In case you're asking why 21 million, it's fundamentally in light of the fact that that is what's composed in the source code.)

The top on Bitcoin generation is there to guarantee that Bitcoin wouldn't ever be hyperinflated.

It's even intended to be created consistently: the reward framework passes significantly every 210,000 squares added to the chain (i.e., like clockwork), with the SHA-256 issues notwithstanding differing in trouble contingent upon the measure of mineworkers—more excavators mean more difficult issues to guarantee that not very numerous bitcoins get delivered at the same time.

Anticipating from this pattern, the last bitcoin is assessed to be mined around the year 2140. To place things in context, there are around 16.74 million bitcoins in presence at the season of composing.

That less and less bitcoins can be mined as time passes by drives up the enthusiasm of the general population in the cash, since irregularity is attractive and exceptionally attractive.

This builds the estimation of Bitcoin, in light of the fact that it works utilizing a system—the bigger the system, the more noteworthy utilize you can escape Bitcoin.

Free Market Activity Affects Bitcoin Value Directly

The market estimation of Bitcoin—that is, the cash that individuals will pay for it—takes after a similar old essential request and supply run: an appeal builds its cost and a low request diminishes it.

Before we go in any further, simply recall that the benefit of something isn't the same as its value; esteem is the thing that individuals see an item is worth, while cost is the thing that they pay for it. All things considered, esteem and cost go as an inseparable unit: the cost of something is straightforwardly identified with its esteem and the other way around.

As per an article in the Economist, the expanding pattern in the cost of Bitcoin is the thing that drives individuals to put resources into it.

Individuals are contributing in light of the fact that they trust that, following the pattern up until this point, they would have the capacity to offer their Bitcoins at a substantially higher cost later on—which the article contends is an ideal case of the more prominent trick hypothesis.

Fundamentally, the more noteworthy trick hypothesis expresses that the cost of an item is resolved not by its characteristic esteem, but rather by the convictions and desires that the shoppers put on the item.

From this point of view, the surging cost of Bitcoin serves not to build its real esteem, but rather to render it superfluous.

The market is driving the cost of Bitcoin up in view of developing conviction that it will be worth more later on, not on the grounds that they think its esteem is expanding after some time. Nonetheless, a few people contend that the surge in Bitcoin costs that the previous year has seen isn't characteristic of it being an air pocket.

In the Bitcoin site itself, it contends that it isn't an air pocket, refering to that air pockets are misleadingly overvaluations of an item which has a tendency to adjust itself in the end.

It refers to its generally little and youthful market as the purpose behind the unpredictability in Bitcoin costs—that "decisions in view of individual human activity by a huge number of market members is the reason at Bitcoin's cost to vacillate as the market looks for value revelation."

It contends that the instability of Bitcoin costs are because of many powers, for example,

• Loss of trust in Bitcoin

• A huge distinction amongst esteem and cost not founded on the basics of the Bitcoin economy

• Increased press scope fortifying theoretical request

• Fear of vulnerability

• And antiquated nonsensical richness and avarice

Accordingly, Bitcoin is contending that its developing costs can be ascribed to an ever increasing number of individuals finding the item progressively justified regardless of their cash in light of its utility, in this manner approving its esteem.

Thus, in rundown: Bitcoin's utility and shortage gives it esteem, however its costs appear to send contradicting signals in the matter of whether it's really significant or not.

With an ever increasing number of individuals starting to demonstrate enthusiasm for Bitcoin, maybe we are scarcely touching the most superficial layer of what its actual esteem might be.

Chapter 2: Diverse Techniques To Acquire Bitcoin

There are a wide range of strategies to procuring bitcoins, and in this guide, we will demonstrate to you the most mainstream techniques for getting yourself a few units of the world's most prominent digital currency.

Get Some Bitcoins

Purchasing bitcoins is an exceptionally basic and clear process. You can just go to a bitcoin trade site, for example, Coinbase or Kraken, and trade your US Dollars, British Pounds, Euros, Canadian Dollars, and other upheld monetary forms (this will rely upon the stage) into some bitcoins.

Obviously, with the consistently expanding estimation of bitcoin, this is simpler said than done.

At the present time, you can hope to spend more than $10,000 for a solitary bitcoin! Fortunately you don't need to purchase an entire bitcoin. Each bitcoin can be separated into 100 million units called Satoshis (named after Bitcoin organizer, Satoshi Nakamoto).

This implies you can purchase a couple of thousand Satoshis for a couple of dollars. While this won't make you rich, you can at any rate discover how bitcoins and digital currency functions.

Here are a portion of the best places where you can purchase bitcoins:

Digital currency Exchanges

There are a lot of stages where you can purchase and offer digital currency. The most prevalent ones that have been around a couple of years are Coinbase, Kraken, Gemini, Coinmama, and CEX.io.

You'll need to do some exploration, be that as it may, if your state or nation is upheld and what monetary standards and installment techniques they acknowledge as every stage would have their own principles and controls.

The exchange expenses included will likewise change in every stage so you'll certainly need to glance around to locate the best digital currency trade that would suit your bitcoin needs.

Money Exchanges

On the off chance that you need to maintain a strategic distance from bitcoin trade stages and pay straightforwardly in real money (or another installment technique that is mainstream in your neighborhood), money trades like LocalBitcoin or Wall of Coins. These stages enable you to exchange straightforwardly with someone else.

There are no costly exchange charges included. In any case, they may charge an expense for fruitful exchanges. We would recommend that you search for a stage that offers an escrow administration to ensure the vender doesn't flee with your well deserved money!

Exchange Your Other Cryptocurrencies For Bitcoin

On the off chance that you have an advanced wallet loaded with different digital forms of money, you can without much of a stretch exchange these for bitcoins. You can go to destinations like ShapeShift.io which enables you to rapidly exchange your non-bitcoin cryptographic money to bitcoins.

You don't require a record to make an exchange. Essentially enter the sum you wish to change over or exchange, your bitcoin address, and your digital currency discount address. That is it! You'll have your new bitcoins in almost no time.

Get Paid With Bitcoins

Getting paid with bitcoins isn't a convoluted procedure by any means. You essentially need your own particular bitcoin wallet so you can begin getting installments. First of all, you can make a free online wallet on Blockchain.info or Coinbase.

All you require is a substantial email deliver to join and start getting installments! Once your wallet is set up, you can either create a QR code or utilize the long alphanumeric deliver and send it to the individual you wish to get bitcoins from.

Here are a few thoughts on how you can get paid with bitcoins:

Work For Bitcoins

There are a wide range of sorts of work you can do to get paid in bitcoin. It doesn't make a difference on the off chance that you work on the web or disconnected as making and accepting bitcoin installments is so straightforward you don't generally require specialized know-how to do it.

Solopreneurs discover this installment technique a lot more helpful as they don't have to hold up 24-48 hours (or more for global specialists) to get bank exchanges from their customers. They can get their installment, compensation, or wages in only a couple of minutes.

It's a major alleviation to specialists knowing they don't have to hold up in limbo, uncertain in the event that they will get paid for their diligent work or not. Managers or customers likewise like not paying those extravagant bank expenses for doing exchanges particularly to specialists or consultants abroad.

With bitcoin installments, they get the chance to spare a lot of cash just in bank charges alone!

Offer Products Or Services

Regardless of whether you are an online shop or a physical store, you can get installments in bitcoin. With a developing group of bitcoin clients, will undoubtedly get new and rehash clients who will work with you basically in light of the fact that you're ground breaking enough to acknowledge bitcoin installments.

The additional advantage to clients is they can without much of a stretch send you installments straight from their bitcoin wallets while you get their installments in a split second. It's extremely a win-win circumstance for both you and your clients!

For online shops, you can utilize modules or contents to begin tolerating bitcoin installments on your website. In case you're uncertain of how you can do this present, it's best to enlist a designer to ensure it's set up right (you don't need those bitcoin installments going elsewhere!).

At the point when your clients go to your checkout page, they'll see the bitcoin alternative and select that on the off chance that they need to pay utilizing bitcoins.

For nearby shops like lodgings, eateries, bars, bistros, blossom shops, basic supplies, and so forth., in the event that you need to get bitcoin installments face to face, you should simply print your wallet's QR code and stick it close to your money enlist.

At the point when your clients are prepared to pay, just direct them to the QR code, have them filter it on their cell phones, enter the sum they have to pay, hit Send, and sit tight for your bitcoins to arrive.

Oh, and keep in mind to include a mammoth 'Bitcoin Accepted Here' sign at the passage to welcome the bitcoin group to come inside! To pull in significantly more bitcoin clients, add your business to Coinmap and other comparative locales where the bitcoin group hangs out and looks for places where they can spend their bitcoins!

Get Tips From Customers

You don't should be in the administration business to get tips. In the event that you have a blog, you can set up a bitcoin installment door where your dependable fans and perusers can tip you on the off chance that they so want.

Try not to disparage the liberality of your group of onlookers particularly in the event that you create content that gives a great deal of significant worth to them. Give it a shot – you could possibly be astounded to see some bitcoins on your wallet following a couple of days!

Finish Small Tasks On Websites

There are currently a lot of locales on the Internet that offer free bitcoins (normally only a, little part of it) for each errand you finish. A few sites expect you to finish reviews, watch recordings, tap on advertisements, answer questions, agree to accept trial offers, download portable applications, play web based recreations, allude companions, shop on the web, and the sky is the limit from there. Installment is typically brisk and simple.

A few stages simply require your bitcoin wallet address while others expect you to join and make a record. While it's actual these occupations are for the most part little and should be possible in almost no time, procuring just a couple of hundred or thousand Satoshis at once may not be justified, despite all the trouble particularly in the event that you esteem your opportunity. However, in the event that you have nothing better to would and you like to encounter direct the delights of owning digital currency, at that point you have a lot of miniaturized scale entrusting locales to look over.

Join Bitcoin Faucets

Bitcoin fixtures are simply sites that give away free Satoshis at set time interims. These locales acquire an enormous measure of movement from individuals needing to get free bitcoins so expect heaps of rivalry and, contingent upon where the fixture is facilitated, moderate stacking times.

A few spigots give away Satoshis with no work included, that is, you simply need the webpage up on your program, while some expect you to tackle little errands previously you gain your Satoshis (much like the miniaturized scale entrusting sites we've talked about in the past segment).

Locales like these are a noteworthy time deplete also so it's truly up to you in the event that you can bear to trade your valuable time for a couple of Satoshis.

Mine Your Own Bitcoin

Bitcoin excavators assume a critical part in the Bitcoin organize. Without mineworkers, there would be no new bitcoins, and no exchanges would be affirmed. Bitcoin mineworkers are so imperative to the Bitcoin environment that they are legitimately compensated with bitcoins for their diligent work. Notwithstanding, bitcoin mining isn't as gainful as it appears.

At the point when Bitcoin was still in its earliest stages, excavators were getting paid 50 bitcoins for each square mined. Be that as it may, each 210,000 hinders (this is around 4 years), the reward is divided. So this implies the underlying 50 bitcoins was divided into 25 bitcoins.

Furthermore, now, at this specific point in time, the piece remunerate is down to 12.5 bitcoins. On the off chance that you consider the cost for one bitcoin at the present time (well finished $10,000), this is still is an extremely alluring prize in reality. What's more, specialists anticipate the cost will keep on going up as the quantity of bitcoins in presence gradually go up, as well, and the interest for more bitcoins keep on increasing.

Mining bitcoins isn't a simple occupation, much like some other physical mining work in reality. Bitcoin diggers may not get grimy from sediment and mud, but rather their effective PCs do.

The trouble in mining new squares has gone up so much that individual mineworkers are discovering it to a great degree hard to fathom complex cryptographic capacities all alone. A wide range of mineworkers or mining bunches contend to find another square and the mining trouble are at greatly abnormal states now.

Most, if not all, diggers are compelled to work in mining pools where a few mineworkers cooperate as a gathering to add new exchanges to the blockchain. At the point when another piece is mined, the reward is part as indicated by the work every mineworker's PC has done.

Mining bitcoins doesn't come modest. You can't simply utilize any PC as illuminating cryptographic capacities will take such an extensive amount your PC's preparing power.

Not even a top of the line workstation or PC can carry out the activity any longer – it's extremely that hard to mine new bitcoin squares today!

Regardless of whether you join mining pools, you'll have to contribute a great deal of cash to purchase the correct equipment. First and foremost, an intense CPU (Computer Processing Unit) and GPU (Graphical Processing Unit) were adequate to mine new squares. Be that as it may, as the trouble of mining bitcoins have gone up, all the more preparing power was required.

Today, an ASIC (Application Specific Integrated Circuit) chip is viewed as the best way to prevail with regards to mining. A bitcoin-mining ASIC chip is outlined particularly to mine bitcoins. It can't do some other errand separated from mining bitcoins.

While this might be seen as a drawback for a few, recall that mining is a difficult activity. You require every one of the assets you can use to locate the following exchange piece so you can add it to the blockchain and get remunerated bitcoins all the while. Proficient mineworkers discover this equipment capable than different innovations utilized as a part of the past.

Likewise, it's not as power eager as other equipment out there. It will even now devour a lot of energy, nonetheless, so consider that in case you're stressed over your power bills.

On the off chance that you are set up to purchase the innovation to mine bitcoins and pay all the more exorbitant power charges, at that point mining bitcoins will be an incredible route for you to obtain this specific cryptographic money.

In any case, we'd get a kick out of the chance to state this isn't work for the uninitiated. It's best to leave this errand to the specialists or those with a top to bottom learning of how bitcoin mining functions. As we've indicated you in this guide, there are numerous ways you can get bitcoins that don't require a solid speculation of both time and cash.

In the following part, we'll broadly expound on bitcoin mining, and you'll see with your own eyes if this is something you need to get engaged with.

Chapter 3: Bitcoin Mining – Everything You Need To Know About Bitcoin Mining

In this guide, we'll cover everything there is to think about Bitcoin mining so you can see whether this is something that you might want to do as such you can get what's coming to you of bitcoins.

Bitcoin has been in the news a ton these days, and its present cost is a wellspring important to many individuals around the globe. A couple of years prior, many individuals marked Bitcoin as a trick, yet now it is seen, alongside different cryptographic forms of money, as the eventual fate of cash.

Cryptographic forms of money, as virtual or advanced monetary standards, have no physical properties and should be 'mined' electronically.

Before we go into subtle elements, we'd jump at the chance to characterize first the most widely recognized terms utilized as a part of Bitcoin mining so you can without much of a stretch see how this very specialized process functions.

Bitcoin Mining Terms You Should Get To Know

Piece: The information identified with exchanges is put away on a page known as a square.

Bitcoins Per Block: This is the quantity of bitcoins remunerated to excavators for each piece mined and added to the blockchain. The underlying prize per square was 50 bitcoins yet every 210,000 hinders, the reward is partitioned by 2. As of now, the reward sits at 12.5 bitcoins per piece.

Bitcoin Difficulty: With an expanding number of mineworkers, Bitcoin mining likewise increments in trouble. The perfect normal mining time characterized by the system is 10 minutes for every piece.

Power Rate: To ascertain the amount you're winning, you have to check your electric bill. This can enable you to judge how much power is expended

by your digging PC as an end-result of your bitcoin income. It is safe to say that you are making a benefit, equaling the initial investment or losing? These are vital inquiries all excavators need to ask themselves.

Hash: In Bitcoin mining, a hash can be viewed as an issue identified with science. The mining machine needs to understand it to gain rewards.

Hash Rate: The time it takes to take care of these hash issues is called Hash Rate. Hash rate increments with the quantity of excavators on the Bitcoin arrange. MH/s (Mega hash every second), GH/s (Giga hash every second), TH/s (Terra hash every second) and PH/s (Peta hash every second) are a portion of the units that are utilized as a part of estimating hash rates.

Pool Fees: Miners join a pool for mining known as a 'mining pool.' Like regular mining, diggers here mine together as it encourages them take care of those intricate hash issues speedier. You need to pay expenses to the pool so it can proceed with its operations. At the point when bitcoins are at last mined, they are circulated to excavators as for their hash rates.

Power Consumption: Not each mining machine devours a similar measure of power. So before getting yourself a costly machine, you should check first how much power it will devour.

Time allotment: This is a span that you have to characterize yourself to perceive the amount you're mining. For instance, you characterize a time span of 45 days. This implies following 45 days, you'll figure what number of bitcoins you've mined amid this period. Characterizing a time period can enable you to check whether you are creating pretty much than your kindred diggers.

Bitcoin Mining Hardware Commonly Used By Miners

CPU (Computer Processing Unit):

In the first place, bitcoin mining was staggeringly simple and could be effectively mined on customary work area CPUs. Be that as it may, as the quantity of mineworkers expanded, bitcoin mining on CPU turned out to be more troublesome and caused PC hard drives to come up short.

GPU (Graphical Processing Unit):

With a surge in the quantity of diggers on the system, the utilization of GPUs began to pick up fame when individuals acknowledged they were more effective for bitcoin mining.

Some progressed GPUs even enabled excavators to expand their mining profitability 50-100 times better in contrast with CPU mining. Individuals likewise began adjusting their BIOS settings to augment their prizes. Nvidia and ATI's cards shot to prominence thus.

FPGA (Field-Programmable Gate Array):

FPGA is an incorporated circuit made with the target of performing bitcoin mining. GPU mining was ending up being not all that productive for everybody as a result of rising power costs. FPGA was intended to expend less power, thus diggers moved from GPUs to FPGAs.

ASIC (Application-Specific Integrated Circuit):

With the entry of ASIC innovation, FPGA was overwhelmed as the essential equipment utilized as a part of bitcoin mining. ASIC is a PC chip that is utilized exclusively to mine of cryptographic forms of money like bitcoins or different coins that utilization the SHA-256 calculation.

Dissimilar to other mining equipment, ASICs can't be utilized to do undertakings other than mining. At the present time, this is the highest quality level which mineworkers swear by as these effective chips tackle more issues in less time while devouring less power also.

The Role Of Mining In The Creation Of New Bitcoins

You can claim bitcoins utilizing a couple of techniques. The most effortless path is to get some bitcoins on a Bitcoin trade stage however, obviously, bitcoin costs are so high now that you'll have to make a sizeable venture.

The other strategy isn't to utilize any cash and rather essentially mine bitcoins utilizing PC equipment.

It's essential to note here that the fundamental and basic motivation behind mining is the creation or arrival of new bitcoins which can be then accessible on the system.

As of now, around 16 million bitcoins have just been mined out of the conceivable 21 million bitcoins that can ever be made.

What Is The Blockchain?

Dissimilar to typical money exchanges being affirmed and controlled through banks, cryptographic forms of money's value-based information shows up an open record known as the 'blockchain'.

Each square can be said as a page that contains the information of exchanges. That is the reason it is called as blockchain. Mining affirms these exchanges on a blockchain.

Excavators likewise run cryptographic hash on squares. A hash requires complex calculations.

These hashes are critical in light of the fact that they influence a square to secure. Once a piece has been acknowledged in the blockchain then it can't be changed. Mineworkers secretly approve these exchanges.

For their assistance, diggers are compensated bitcoins. 'Evidence of work' is the term begat for the help of excavators in approving exchanges.

What Exactly Is Bitcoin Mining?

The term 'mining' is regularly utilized with normal assets like gold, silver, and different minerals. These assets are restricted in supply and are along these lines exceptionally significant wares, much like Bitcoin.

Thus, 'mining' is the term utilized by Bitcoin originator, Satoshi Nakamoto, on the grounds that excavators will basically be diving deep into the Bitcoin system to mine those valuable coins.

Bitcoin excavators may not get grimy staring them in the face and knees to mine bitcoins, yet with the expanding trouble of tackling complex cryptographic hash capacities, they should be!

The Bitcoin mining process makes these 2 comes about: the first is it secures and checks exchanges that are occurring on the Bitcoin organize, and the second is it makes new bitcoins.

Bitcoin mining includes utilizing the SHA-256 calculation. SHA remains for Secure Hashing Algorithm which is a computational calculation that is utilized for encryption.

Since Bitcoin is a decentralized kind of cash, which means no focal body or specialist offers authorizations to diggers, anybody with access to power and a mining machine can mine bitcoin.

In any case, these mining machines are themselves expensive as you require specific PC chips to mine bitcoin productively, as those perplexing hash capacities excavators need to unravel turn out to be more convoluted after some time.

In the good 'ol days, you could utilize your PC's CPU (PC preparing unit) and GPU (illustrations handling unit) to take care of hash issues, yet today the issues are so convoluted, mineworkers are setting up costly apparatuses and shaping mining gatherings to pool their PC assets!

Singular diggers are left with no decision yet to join mining bunches in light of the fact that their individual machines just can't deal with the troublesome workload.

Bitcoin Mining And Mining Difficulty

PCs engaged with bitcoin mining attempt to take care of complex numerical issues that are close unthinkable for an individual to understand. Are these issues winding up progressively troublesome, as well as tedious for PCs as these take a ton of time, and electric power, to fathom.

Truth be told, master mineworkers assess that around $150,000 worth of power is utilized every day by Bitcoin diggers everywhere throughout the world!

By and large, it takes around 10 minutes for Bitcoin excavators to locate another square with each piece containing around 2,000 exchanges. These 10 minutes is the time required for bitcoin exchanges to be approved by the system and to frame another square.

Thus, another square is made each time these unpredictable issues get comprehended. This procedure is all the more normally known as 'Verification Of Work,' and this dispenses with the likelihood of having just a couple of mineworkers mine all the rest of the bitcoins for themselves.

Since Bitcoin's system is decentralized without a focal body checking the exchanges, this self-represented framework implies every mineworker is a fundamental piece of the framework. Without mineworkers, there would be no bitcoins, plain and straightforward. Because of the imperative part mineworkers' play in the Bitcoin organize, they are compensated in a couple of ways.

In the first place, the exchange expenses that clients pay for each bitcoin exchange is sent to the excavators. Furthermore, the system remunerates each triumphant excavator a set number of bitcoins; the second reward is vital in light of the fact that this is the main way that new bitcoins are made. Along these lines, diggers need to keep mining with the goal that more bitcoins are made and discharged into the system.

In 2009, when the main Bitcoin square was mined by Satoshi Nakamoto himself, the reward was 50 bitcoins for each piece.

Notwithstanding, the reward is decreased considerably every 210,000 pieces or around 4 years.

This implies 210,000 pieces after the beginning (or first since forever) square was mined, the mineworker who effectively mined the 210,001st piece was just compensated 25 bitcoins; this happened on 28th November 2012.

At that point another 210,000 pieces later, on ninth July 2016, the reward was again split, this time into 12.5 bitcoins. It is normal that at some point in the year 2021, the following 210,000 squares will be finished and the reward will drop down to 6.25 bitcoins.

Another fascinating thing to note is that while the prizes are getting littler and littler, the mining trouble is expanding. There's significantly more rivalry now, and solo excavators discover it close to difficult to locate a solitary piece without anyone else. Joining mining bunches enable a few excavators to pool their assets, yet this likewise implies they are sharing the bitcoin compensate among themselves.

Bitcoin Cloud Mining – An Alternative To Joining Mining Pools?

Be careful! Bitcoin cloud mining stages are brimming with Ponzi-style defrauding operations. While some consider this to be an incredible other option to mining pools, there are just a couple of authentic cloud mining operations.

In principle, cloud mining is the ideal answer for individuals who need to mine bitcoins without purchasing their own particular mining PCs and joining a pool.

They don't have to stress over power and the various issues that genuine excavators need to manage. To put it plainly, you should simply pay up the membership charge and sit tight for your bitcoin income to be sent to your wallet. Sounds incredible, correct?

Many individuals are pulled in to this model, and obviously, con artists and cheats are prepared to loan them a hand and assuage them of their cash.

Is Bitcoin Mining Profitable?

This million dollar question will find you various solutions. Some would urge you to simply ahead and mine, while others will let you know the

time to mine bitcoins has passed. With Bitcoin costs persistently breaking records and achieving untouched highs, the speculation might be justified, despite all the trouble.

Be that as it may, Bitcoin is such an unpredictable digital money, and we can never anticipate the course its cost will take, so it's a tremendous hazard for diggers too when the value drops.

At the point when this happens, the best thing for excavators to do is to clutch their bitcoins and sit tight at the cost to backpedal up again before offering their bitcoins to anxious purchasers.

Chapter 4: Bitcoin Storing – How To Store Your Bitcoin And Other Cryptocurrency Safely

Guarding your bitcoins from prying eyes, malevolent bots, programmers and your regular cheats, isn't simple. Everybody needs a bit of bitcoin these days, it appears.

On the off chance that individuals know you've put resources into Bitcoin in the good 'ol days, regardless you have your speculation with you, at that point they know you're truly sitting over a fortune. We would prefer not to sound vile, yet it's simply tragic an unavoidable truth that a few people will do anything for cash or for this situation, bitcoins.

There are numerous ways you can guard your valuable computerized fortune. Much the same as your paper cash, you can store distinctive measures of bitcoin in various kinds of wallets. Some are 'hot' wallets while some are viewed as 'icy.' You'll take in more about these kinds of wallets as we experience each of them in this guide.

It's imperative to specify here that when we say 'guarding the bitcoins,' we're really alluding to keeping the 'private key' safe. Inside your wallet, your bitcoins would have a related address, and each bitcoin address is made out of an 'open key' and a 'private key.'

People in general key is THE bitcoin address itself, and it can be imparted to anyone. General society key can be contrasted with an email address. Everyone who knows your email address can send you messages.

The private key is undifferentiated from your email secret word. Without a secret word, nobody can read your email. Similarly, without a private key, you can't make an exchange to send bitcoins to another client. This is the reason keeping the private key safe is of most extreme significance.

In the event that programmers get hold of your private key, they can send ALL your bitcoins to their own particular records.

In view of the way Bitcoin is planned, there's no chance to get for you to know where your bitcoins would be sent and there is totally zero shot of recovering any bitcoins. Bitcoin's most appealing highlights, for example, close moment exchanges, unknown and irreversible exchanges are additionally your greatest concerns if your private keys get stolen.

Once your bitcoins are stolen and exchanged to another client, you truly have no other decision however to acknowledge the reality and proceed onward. There is nothing else you can do.

So how about we proceed onward to how you can keep your private keys, and your bitcoins, safe from programmers and criminals.

Online Wallets

The simplest method to begin with bitcoins is by getting an online wallet. You don't need bitcoins yet to get your own wallet. You can essentially go to locales like Blockchain.info, Coinbase.com, and other bitcoin trade stages to make your first wallet.

On the web or web wallets are awesome for those simply getting their feet wet with bitcoins and the individuals who don't have a sizeable stock of bitcoins yet.

They are anything but difficult to setup, they're extremely helpful, and you can get to them from anyplace with an Internet association. Online wallets are 'hot wallets' for this very reason – anybody can get to your wallet, as well!

Actually, what's much more terrible is that most web wallets store your private keys on their servers so if the stage is hacked, at that point your bitcoins are on a par with gone.

In like manner, if a genuine specialized glitch occurs on the site, your private keys could be traded off or completely gone. There's additionally the genuine danger of having your record restricted or suspended by the stage. You may unconsciously conflict with the site's terms of administration or something comparable, and they can close your record down, and your private keys, for eternity.

On the off chance that you have a critical bitcoin stash, at that point it's ideal on the off chance that you move it to a more secure 'cool' wallet that is not associated with the Internet. Not having control over your bitcoins is a terrifying idea and one that you shouldn't take a risk on.

While there are characteristic dangers to online wallets, it's not all awful particularly in the event that you make exchanges much of the time. You can simply store a couple of bitcoins in your online wallet for those standard exchanges and keep the rest in a more secure wallet.

Along these lines despite everything you'll get the chance to encounter the accommodation of an online wallet while having significant serenity that an expansive level of your bitcoins are out of damage's way.

Mobile Wallets

Much the same as online wallets, versatile application wallets are additionally 'hot' wallets since you can without much of a stretch access your bitcoins anyplace you have an Internet association. Out of the considerable number of wallets on this guide, versatile wallets are the most helpful. It may not be the most secure, but rather nobody can deny its comfort.

You can send bitcoin installments to any vendor on the web or disconnected. Some web wallets have a portable partner. For example, both Blockchain.info and Coinbase portable wallets are matched up to your web wallets which is extremely exceptionally advantageous as the two wallets synchronize consequently so you can see your adjust when you sign in or get to either wallet.

This comfort is decisively why more neighborhood organizations ought to acknowledge bitcoin installments. The Bitcoin people group is developing at an exponential rate, and these wise clients would introduce versatile wallets on their iPhones and Android cell phones.

There's presumably no simpler route for them to pay than simply filtering your bitcoin address' QR code and hitting that Send catch to pay for your items or administrations!

Nonetheless, not all things are great with versatile wallets. For example, your private keys can even now be gotten to by programmers whether it's saved money on an outsider server or your cell phone.

In the event that you lose your cell phone or it gets harmed, you could likewise possibly lose all your bitcoins and other cryptographic money in the event that you didn't make reinforcement duplicates of your private keys and put away them some place safe.

The most ideal approach to exploit a portable wallet is by just exchanging what you require from a more secure wallet (like an equipment wallet) to your versatile wallet. Along these lines regardless of whether you lose your telephone, and you can't recuperate your private keys on there, at that point you won't lose all your bitcoins.

Desktop Wallets

The third kind of wallet you can use to store your bitcoins moderately securely is a work area wallet. It's essentially a work area application where you store your private keys in. The most well known one, however not generally the most down to earth one, is Bitcoin Core.

When you introduce the product, you have to ensure you have more than (at least 150gb) free circle space as it will naturally download the whole blockchain going back to 2009!

You can't not download the blockchain as Bitcoin Core won't process any exchange unless the whole record has been downloaded to your framework. When it's been downloaded, you would then be able to begin sending and accepting bitcoins to your wallet.

On the off chance that you don't have a lot of plate space to save, nor the transmission capacity to download such a huge document, at that point here's some uplifting news for you - Bitcoin Core isn't the main work area wallet accessible these days.

You've really got a lot of decisions to browse, for example, Electrum, Bither, Armory, and the sky is the limit from there, which don't expect you to download the blockchain as it utilizes SPV (Simple Payment Verification) innovation.

Work area wallets are generally simple to utilize, and it's more secure than a web or portable wallet since you can simply detach your PC from the Internet to stay away from programmers from getting in your framework and taking your private keys.

Obviously, it's not as helpful as a web or versatile wallet, yet at any rate you have full control over your private keys. You can keep a reinforcement duplicate of the keys just on the off chance that your PC gets stolen, tainted with an infection or for all time harmed.

On the off chance that you don't reinforcement your private keys, you could lose all your bitcoins in a matter of moments.

Paper Wallets

It may sound unusual at first to store your computerized digital money in a paper wallet. You're likely going to inquire as to why anybody would do that when bitcoin doesn't exist physically.

Bitcoin and paper may not appear like a match made in paradise, but rather when you consider it, they really do. All things considered, in some capacity in any event.

Paper wallets are a type of 'cool stockpiling' since Internet programmers won't ever get the chance to hack into your little bit of paper. There are a lot of talented programmers who can figure out how to get to most PCs and servers, yet we're almost certain paper isn't one of them.

Your bitcoins might be sheltered from programmers yet not from disconnected cheats. In the event that you don't deal with your paper wallet, on the off chance that you abandon it lying around in

unsecured spots, at that point you're actually giving somebody the keys to your fortune!

Water is likewise something you ought to consider when utilizing paper wallets. Putting away your wallets in zip locks and other water safe compartments should help defeat this issue.

Paper wallets are not as advantageous as portable or web wallets, but rather they are certainly more secure. You can print both your open and private keys and conceal it some place safe like a wellbeing store box.

Paper wallets are the best sort of wallet for putting away your private keys for drawn out stretches of time.

In the event that you don't expect to touch your bitcoins for quite a long time or years, at that point you can make paper wallets. Obviously, much the same as we've suggested in past segments, it's best to keep a couple of bitcoins (just what you can stand to lose) in more advantageous wallets so you can keep sending and accepting bitcoins. Whatever remains of your private keys can go in the paper wallet.

Hardware Wallets

There's an accord in the Bitcoin people group that equipment wallets are the most secure bitcoin wallets and something each genuine Bitcoin financial specialist and fan ought to think about purchasing. Not at all like the other wallet composes we've shrouded so far in this guide, equipment wallets are generally costly.

Obviously, in the event that you have an extensive number of bitcoins to secure, at that point it's extremely a little cost to pay for protecting your fortune. Most equipment wallets bolster a large group of cryptographic forms of money so on the off chance that you've put resources into non-

bitcoin monetary forms as well, at that point you'll observe this sort of wallet to be an incredible buy.

Equipment wallets are essentially effective and solid USB sticks which you connect to your PC when making a bitcoin or digital money exchange. When you're set, just evacuate the wallet and store it some place safe.

A one of a kind security include on equipment wallets is the capacity to produce private keys disconnected which implies that it's less defenseless against programmer assaults. These durable little gadgets enable you to carry your private keys anyplace with you without dread of having it presented to the outside world.

Setup is additionally brisk and simple with equipment wallets. Contingent upon the wallet, you can allot a PIN code, secret word, or recuperation seed words which you can use to validate your entrance and recoup your bitcoins in the event that your wallet is lost or decimated.

Just on the off chance that you get some type of amnesia and overlook your recuperation points of interest, you ought to record your mystery subtle elements and shroud it some place just you know. Something else, on the off chance that somebody discovers it, either unintentionally or by plan, at that point your bitcoins and whatever cryptographic money you have on there will soon be gone.

Equipment wallets are astounding for putting away all your digital forms of money securely. Regardless of whether you have a sizeable accumulation of computerized cash or not, you never need to stress if your wallet will be hacked and your cash stolen.

Your private keys are moderately protected. You simply need to ensure your memory never comes up short you, and you'll recall forget where you've shrouded your wallet reinforcements!

To total up this guide, the best wallet for your bitcoins and digital forms of money are really a mix of various wallets. Utilize hard wallets or paper wallets for long haul stockpiling, work area wallets for medium-term stockpiling, and web and portable wallets for here and now stockpiling and regular exchanges.

Chapter 5: Exchanging And Selling Your Bitcoin For Profit

Exchanging and offering your bitcoin can be an extremely beneficial action. You most likely know somebody or caught wind of somebody who purchased bitcoins in the good 'ol days when they were worth nothing, and wound up offering each bitcoin for a large number of dollars!

Or then again you may know individuals who take part in exchanging bitcoins and are benefitting pleasantly also. It may appear to be simple, however truly, exchanging bitcoins isn't for everybody.

Novices are particularly encouraged to take alert and to be rationally and fiscally prepared before venturing out into this energizing high-hazard and high-remunerate world. When exchanging, it's presence of mind to take after the 'purchase low and offer high' system so you can make a benefit.

You would prefer not to offer at a value lower than when you purchased in light of the fact that you'll be offering at a misfortune. In any case, every one of these sounds simple on paper.

In reality, when you're managing bitcoins that is worth hundreds, thousands or even a huge number of dollars, in the event that you don't have the correct mentality and the money related teach, you could freeze effectively.

Particularly in case you're exchanging bitcoins that speak to as long as you can remember reserve funds, your retirement finance, or your children's school educational cost!

Bitcoin Trading Strategies

Good judgment and poise should outweigh eagerness and the possibility of benefitting a great many dollars in a solitary day. Here are some bitcoin exchanging techniques to manage you in the exchanging scene.

Practice First

Taking in the intricate details of bitcoin exchanging is incredible, yet knowing just hypothesis is not the same as certifiable application. Some bitcoin trades offer a demo account where you can play around and encounter true exchanging utilizing continuous costs.

You'll figure out the scene, in a manner of speaking, and you'll see with your own eyes whether you have the stomach for the high-hazard round of bitcoin exchanging.

Plan Your Strategy

To exchange bitcoins effectively, you need a decent methodology set up. You don't simply aimlessly take after the news and believe that on the grounds that everybody's purchasing bitcoins, at that point you ought to purchase as well.

Have an arrangement set up on what value you should purchase bitcoins at and what cost to offer them at to benefit, and ensure you adhere to that arrangement. This implies keeping your frenzy under control at whatever point you see the value drop.

Contribute Small Amounts

As a feature of your training or preparing system, you should begin little and don't bet everything when you first exchange. It is fine to lose all your 'cash' in a demo account, however when it's genuine cash, you would prefer not to hazard losing tremendous totals on your first day.

Control Your Emotions

It's ordinary to feel frightened at the main trace of losing your cash. Be that as it may, as you definitely know Bitcoin is exceptionally unstable, and in a solitary day, the cost can go around hundreds or thousands of dollars. In any case, the inverse is additionally valid. The cost can simply go up in the following hour or somewhere in the vicinity.

On the off chance that you hold your feelings within proper limits and think legitimately, you also can profit with Bitcoin exchanging.

In any case, on the off chance that you neglect to control your feelings and you let your frenzy defeat you, at that point will undoubtedly lose.

Mainstream Bitcoin Trading Platforms

Since you know some exceptionally helpful Bitcoin exchanging methodologies, it's a great opportunity to find out about the absolute most prevalent exchanging stages for Bitcoin and different cryptographic forms of money.

Coinbase

Coinbase is one of the greatest computerized money trades on the planet today with more than 50 billion dollars of advanced cash traded since 2011. They as of now serve more than 10 million clients situated in 32 nations.

The stage is anything but difficult to utilize, and you can without much of a stretch purchase and exchange your advanced money.

• To start, you need to make a free advanced wallet which you can use to store your cryptographic money.

• Next, you have to connect your ledger, credit or platinum card, so you can trade your nearby money into your preferred digital currency.

• Once your record is set up and subsidized, it's a great opportunity to get some crypto.

You have the alternative to purchase bitcoins, ethereum, and litecoin. You can do this either on their site or their convenient portable application.

Since you are very brave, you can begin exchanging on Coinbase's GDAX (Global Digital Asset Exchange) exchanging stage in spite of the fact that this is equipped towards further developed and experienced brokers.

For apprentices however, it's best to adhere to Coinbase's more amateur benevolent interface. The fortunate thing about Coinbase is that your computerized money is completely safeguarded while your fiat cash (nearby cash) are put away in custodial financial balances. The USD Coinbase wallets of US nationals are secured by FDIC protection, up to a greatest of $250,000.

To offer your bitcoins, ethereum or litecoins, you basically need to show the sum you need to offer and the wallet you're offering from. At that point select the connected financial balance you wish to store your money to.

As of now, Coinbase does not enable the returns of your deal to be sent to a credit or platinum card, so it's critical you interface a financial balance to your Coinbase account.

Kraken

Kraken is a standout amongst the most trusted names in bitcoin and cryptographic money trade since 2011. The organization is additionally thought to be the biggest

bitcoin trade as far as Euro volume and liquidity. Notwithstanding exchanging bitcoins, they additionally exchange US dollars, Canadian dollars, British pounds and Japanese yen.

Numerous global clients cherish Kraken on the grounds that it's extremely available universally and they bolster a wide range of kinds of national monetary standards and digital forms of money.

Kraken offers numerous choices for exchanging. You can without much of a stretch exchange between any of their 17 upheld digital forms of money with Euros, USD, CAD, JPY, and GBP. They offer such a significant number of conceivable exchanging sets, they have a long page devoted only for their expense plan!

To begin with Kraken, you have to make a free record. After you've confirmed your record, you would then be able to support it with money or digital currency and afterward submit a request to purchase bitcoins (or another crypto) on the trade.

At the point when your request ask for is satisfied, you would then be able to pull back your bitcoins/crypto to your wallet. Their web interface is moderately basic when requesting, be that as it may, their exchanging instruments are hearty and are awesome for further developed clients.

To offer bitcoins, you have to send your bitcoins from your wallet to your Kraken record and afterward make another request to offer or exchange them for any of the accessible national monetary standards. Once your request is filled, you would then be able to continue to pull back the money to your connected ledger.

CEX.io

CEX.io is a standout amongst the most well known digital money trade stages today with more than 1 million dynamic clients around the world. In any case, the organization wasn't initially a trade; it was really settled in 2013 as the principal ever cloud mining supplier. While the mining part of the business has since been shut, their trade stage is unmistakably flourishing.

Numerous clients value CEX.io's evaluating straightforwardness. In case you're purchasing bitcoins, they make it so natural for you to perceive how much your $100, $200, $500 or $1000 will get you.

You can likewise effortlessly observe exactly how much bitcoin you can purchase in British Pound, Euro, and Russian Ruble. The purchasing cost is refreshed like clockwork.

To begin, you have to make a record and add subsidizes to it by utilizing your charge card (you can connect any number of Visas to your record), or you can complete a bank exchange, as well. They acknowledge USD, EUR, RUB, GBP, or your nearby cash.

Once the assets are added to your record, you can undoubtedly purchase bitcoins with 1 click. You at that point have the alternative of putting away it in your CEX.io wallet, exchange it or pull back to your own wallet.

Offering bitcoins is likewise simple on CEX.io. Basically have the bitcoins in your record, at that point utilize their convenient purchase/offer area for moment money, or you can put in a request in the Trade segment of the site (you may show signs of improvement conversion standard on the off chance that you exchange).

You can rapidly pull back your income to your Visa or Mastercard and get your assets in a flash. On the other hand, for bigger exchanges, you can pull back through bank exchange or SEPA in case you're in Europe.

Bitstamp

Established in 2011 in the UK, Bitstamp is one of the pioneers in Bitcoin exchanging. They are continually enhancing their administrations, and to date, they permit exchanging of bitcoin, swell, litecoin, ether and bitcoin money. Bitstamp has a decent notoriety overall particularly since they acknowledge exchanges from anybody on the planet.

All real charge cards are acknowledged too, so it makes the stage well disposed to worldwide clients. They additionally guarantee no concealed charges with straightforward volume-based estimating. They ensure that 98% of advanced assets are put away disconnected for security.

Bitstamp does not offer bitcoins themselves. Rather, they give an administration or stage where individuals exchange specifically with each other and purchasers get their bitcoins and venders get their money at the value they need.

To begin with purchasing and offering bitcoins, you should make a Bitstamp account. You at that point need to exchange assets to your record by means of SEPA, wire exchange or Mastercard. When installment is credited, you can put in a moment purchase request which will enable you to consequently purchase bitcoins at the most reduced cost offered on the Bitstamp showcase.

A moment choice to purchase bitcoins is by putting in a breaking point request wherein you can set the value you will purchase bitcoins.

To offer bitcoins, you have to stack your Bitstamp account with bitcoins first. Once you've done this, you would then be able to submit a moment pitch request to naturally offer your bitcoins at the most noteworthy cost offered available.

On the other hand, you can put in an offer breaking point request where you can set the cost at which you will offer your bitcoins. Once your bitcoins are sold, you can continue to pull back your assets in USD or EUR cash.

Bitfinex

Since 2014, Hong Kong-based Bitfinex has been the world's biggest cryptographic money exchanging stage regarding volume. This full-highlighted spot exchanging stage permits exchanges among the real digital currencies, for example, Bitcoin, Ethereum, Litecoin, Money, Dash, Ripple, and that's only the tip of the iceberg. Having such a substantial volume of Bitcoin trades occurring on this stage suggests the best liquidity.

This implies you can exchange an extensive volume of bitcoins at the value you need. Bitfinex's expenses are additionally low when contrasted with other digital money trades on this guide. This is the reason many individuals like exchanging on this stage as more cash goes to their records as opposed to being paid in expenses.

Financing your Bitfinex account isn't as basic as alternate trades however. The best way to store cash is by means of bank wire exchange which can take days. Over the deferral, you'd additionally need to pay Bitfinex a 0.1% of the store sum with a $20 least. Pulling back your dollars is likewise a cerebral pain as they just offer bank wire withdrawals. Your cash may take up to 7 days to post to your record!

To keep away from this burden, exchanging specialists recommend getting your bitcoins or other crypto somewhere else and after that simply exchanging it to your Bitfinex account. For withdrawals, you can pull back your crypto to your wallet and afterward offer it locally. This workaround implies you simply utilize Bitfinex entirely to trade digital forms of money.

It Is Safe To Say That You Are Ready To Start Trading Bitcoins?

There are numerous more bitcoin and digital money trades we've not possessed the capacity to incorporate into this guide. It's best to perform due persistence and research before choosing an exchanging stage. Simply recollect that whichever cryptographic money trade stage you work with, you should dependably move your digital currency to a more secure wallet, for example, an equipment wallet or paper wallet.

Try not to abandon it in your trade's wallet as it's at awesome danger of being stolen by programmers. In the event that you should store some in your online wallet, simply keep the littlest sum you can stand to lose.

Bitcoin is a moderately new type of cash which is simply beginning to pick up footing and overall acknowledgment. With the current exponential development in the estimation of Bitcoin, many individuals are putting resources into this advanced money to ideally procure colossal benefits later on.

In this guide, we will cover the essentials of utilizing bitcoin as a venture methodology. Note that we are alluding to long haul venture here which isn't the same as exchanging bitcoin for here and now benefits.

Putting resources into the very unstable cryptographic money market may not appear like such a smart thought for a few people. Preferably, you'd have nerves of steel, the train and center to overlook here and now picks up, and the persistence to hold your speculation until the point that the perfect time comes.

In case you're extremely resolved to possess a little offer of the crypto-showcase, at that point you ought to in any event know the most reasonable strategies so you can take advantage of your venture.

Bitcoin Investment Methods

Dollar Cost Averaging Method

This methodology is best for amateurs to the contributing scene since you don't have to stress over entering the market at the opportune time.

You don't need to pressure yourself sitting tight at the cost of bitcoin to go down; rather, you simply purchase at standard time interims to spread the hazard and hold/store your bitcoins in a chilly, secure wallet (like a paper wallet or equipment wallet).

For instance, in the event that you have an additional $100 to save each week, you can purchase bitcoins consistently. A little while your $100 may get you more bitcoin, and half a month a similar sum will get you less.

This strategy gives you genuine feelings of serenity since you don't have to stress over the dunks in bitcoin cost.

You simply must be sufficiently trained to take after your standard timetable and purchase when you have to purchase without taking a gander at the bitcoin value diagrams. You don't sit tight at the cost to go down in light of the fact that you see a descending pattern on the diagrams, you simply go ideal out and purchase your bitcoins.

With the dollar cost averaging technique, your benefits will likewise normal out when you choose to offer your bitcoins. It won't not come anyplace near benefits in the event that you contributed utilizing the single amount strategy, yet in the event that you offer at the correct time (when the cost is high), regardless you'll make a solid benefit from your speculation.

Singular amount Investing Method

The singular amount technique is a substantially more hazardous strategy for contributing bitcoins in light of the fact that you will purchase your bitcoins at a solitary value point.

On the off chance that you have $100,000 to contribute, you will, obviously, need to purchase the most number of bitcoins, so you sit tight at the cost to go down. To boost your

speculation, you will be constrained to sit tight at the conceivable most reduced cost before purchasing your bitcoins.

This technique implies you should 'time' the market, so you purchase at simply the correct time. Obviously, this is less demanding said than finished with an unstable ware like bitcoin. The cost shifts so much it's to a great degree hard to foresee when the following value plunge is so you can purchase at that cost.

Endeavoring to time the market can make a great deal of cerebral pain and stress an unpracticed financial specialist. It just brings too much 'what uncertainties' to mind, for example,

'Consider the possibility that I simply hold up a couple of more hours, the cost may go down, and I'd have the capacity to purchase more bitcoins at that point.' Or 'Imagine a scenario where the cost never goes down to the value I need to purchase bitcoins at, I'll never have the capacity to purchase bitcoins.

With regards to auctioning off your single amount interest later on, you may think that its difficult to offer also in light of the fact that you'll be holding up to offer at the perfect time so you can make the most benefit.

You'll endeavor to foresee the most noteworthy value point, and you'll upbraid yourself on the off chance that you sold too early and miss out on the likelihood of substantially more prominent benefit.

The good thing with single amount speculation technique however is whether you figure out how to purchase at the most minimal conceivable cost and offer at the most noteworthy conceivable value, at that point you'll make a substantially greater benefit than if you contributed bitcoins utilizing the dollar cost averaging strategy.

Crypto Hedge Fund Investing Method

On the off chance that you would prefer not to inconvenience yourself with taking in the nuts and bolts of contributing utilizing either the dollar cost averaging strategy or the single amount technique, you may be in an ideal situation putting your cash in a cryptographic money fence stock investments. Notwithstanding, this alternative is most appropriate for individuals who can bear to pay their weighty administration and execution charges.

The administration charge is paid forthright; a few assets require a 2% administration expense so in case you're contributing $100,000, $2,000 of that is heading off to the administration expense which implies just $98,000 will be put resources into digital money.

Likewise, your support investments director will get a level of your benefits. A few administrators require a 20% execution charge so on the off chance that you benefit $50,000 from your venture, $10,000 of that will be paid as a motivating force expense.

The fence investments technique may not suit everybody, but rather on the off chance that you look past the charges, you're in any event taking a gander at a hands-off way to deal with contributing which could turn out to be exceptionally gainful for both you and your support stock investments director.

Methodologies To Succeed In Bitcoin Investing

Putting resources into bitcoin is like putting resources into stocks. Both are high hazard and high reward ventures which, without a doubt, isn't for everybody.

Bitcoin is considerably more unpredictable than stocks so on the off chance that you need to put resources into this digital currency or some other crypto so far as that is concerned, you have to know the accompanying procedures to succeed.

Have A Solid Plan In Place

Try not to contribute aimlessly and don't contribute in light of the fact that everybody you know has purchased bitcoins. When contributing, you need a decent, strong arrangement set up where you draw your entrance point and your leave point.

Your arrangement should be as per the speculation strategy you'll take after. So in the event that you pick the dollar cost averaging strategy, you need a strong arrangement like how much and how frequently you'll be purchasing bitcoins.

For singular amount contributing, you have to know ahead of time at what value you'll be purchasing your bitcoins and purchase at that cost (don't sit tight for it to go any lower). For fence stock investments contributing, you have to consider the charges you have to pay and know the best time to contribute.

Be Prepared For Volatility

This is the main methodology you have to ace. Everybody realizes that bitcoin is a profoundly unstable speculation with costs going all over by many dollars in insignificant minutes. You may contemplate internally you definitely know it will be unpredictable in light of the fact that you've seen the diagrams and the charts and you've honed in a demo bitcoin trade account.

You can deal with the hazard, you let yourself know. Yet, when you have a huge number of genuine dollars on hold, it's an altogether different situation. Particularly in the event that you've endeavored to get those dollars! You may have worked for it for quite a long time or years, and there's an undeniable shot you could lose everything in only a couple of minutes.

The best thing you can do is to not waste time with the plunges by any stretch of the imagination. Simply accomplish something that will enable you to unwind and keep your psyche off bitcoins in light of the fact that on the off chance that you don't, you can actually go insane. Bitcoin contributing resembles an exciting ride; you simply need to hang on ridiculously tight until the point that you get to the finish of the ride!

Don't Panic

Saying this to froze financial specialists is simple, however when you're the terrified one, it's an alternate feeling out and out. The possibility of thousands of dollars down the deplete is sufficient to send anybody to a psychological breakdown which would, obviously, prompt silly choices.

On the off chance that you don't think plainly, you may consider cutting your misfortunes in that spot and afterward without thinking about what will occur in the long haul. On the off chance that you played your cards right, your bitcoins would be worth far beyond when you paid for it. In any case, you're never going to encounter that in the event that you frenzy and offer early.

Keep Perspective

Putting resources into bitcoin is a long haul monetary movement. It's unique in relation to everyday exchanging which includes significantly more specialized examination so a merchant can make a pleasant benefit. When putting resources into bitcoin, you have zoom out of the bitcoin value outlines and take a gander at the general picture. Try not to try taking a gander at the day by day, week after week or month to month graphs since it will bring you only pressure.

Take a gander at how far bitcoin rates have come. From actually a couple of pennies when it initially began to a large number of dollars now. What's more, specialists are stating this

upward pattern will proceed for some, more years to come so on the off chance that you ride out the highs and lows of bitcoin, you'll wind up with an exceptionally pleasant venture portfolio in a couple of years.

Try not to Spend What You Can't Lose

This is presumably the most essential exhortation you have to observe. You definitely know putting resources into profoundly unstable digital currencies can either make you madly rich or bankrupt. In any case, it doesn't need to be these two extremes.

You don't need to contribute your whole fortune or your whole life reserve funds in bitcoin or some other cryptographic money!

The most reasonable thing you can do is to just contribute what you can bear to lose. This implies not spending any cash that you can't stand to lose.

Regardless of whether you contribute utilizing the dollar cost averaging technique, singular amount contributing strategy, or perhaps putting resources into a crypto fence stock investment, don't utilize cash that should be utilized elsewhere.

In the event that you have cash put aside for your retirement, a wellbeing store, a backup stash, or possibly your children's school cash, don't consider touching these assets. Such huge numbers of families have gone to pieces as a result of wrong monetary choices and spent such essential subsidizes on dangerous ventures.

On the off chance that you've accomplished something comparative previously and could escape with it, that is, you've made a few benefits, at that point don't get arrogant and figure you can do likewise with digital money. It's an alternate creature, in a manner of speaking. It's the Wild West of speculations at the present time, and you would prefer not to lose your well deserved cash.

Tolerance And Discipline Are Keys To Success

Bitcoin contributing is a long haul amusement. You should be quiet when the bitcoin cost goes down, and your venture alongside it. On the off chance that you've taken a gander at bitcoin patterns, you'll see it's been in an upward pattern since its initiation in 2009, so you simply need to ride out the troughs until the point when you get to the correct peak where you'll be cheerful to offer your bitcoins.

In the realm of Bitcoin contributing, there'll be numerous troughs and peaks. You simply require the train to clutch your ventures and not get terrified when costs get too low. In like manner, don't get excessively energized when the cost goes up. A strong arrangement, tolerance, and teach will lead you to bitcoin contributing achievement.

Hindsight is Always 20/20

Try not to criticize yourself on the off chance that you purchased at a value significantly higher than the current bitcoin cost. What's more, there's no point getting furious at yourself on the off chance that you sold your bitcoins too soon when the cost goes up after you sold.

Nobody can foresee what's to come. So the best thing for you to do is simply intend to make a clean benefit and not consider the 'what uncertainties' since that is extremely not going to help you by any means.

As is commonly said, insight into the past is dependably 20/20. To place things into point of view, if everybody can see the future, we would all have put resources into bitcoins when it was first presented by Bitcoin organizer, Satoshi Nakamoto.

While numerous on the web and physical shops and organizations have added Bitcoin to their installment alternatives, it's still not as across the board as the Bitcoin people group might want it to be. Most entrepreneurs still incline toward conventional installment techniques as they basically don't know enough about Bitcoin and what they'd escape adding it to their business.

Many don't confide in Bitcoin and its unpredictability. They're most likely reasoning that with such unstable changes in the dollar-bitcoin trade rates, they would presumably wind up losing their benefits. This dread is justifiable, however there have been such a large number of developments these days this truly isn't a worry by any means.

All things considered, some outstanding organizations like Microsoft, Overstock, Expedia, Wikipedia, Wordpress.com, Shopify, thus considerably more, are as of now tolerating Bitcoin installments.

On/Offline Businesses Can Accept Bitcoin Payments

Because Bitcoin is a virtual money that is electronic in nature doesn't imply that disconnected shops can't exploit getting bitcoin installments. For online shops, you can coordinate installment processors, for example, Stripe, Coinbase, Braintree, and that's only the tip of the iceberg, into your web based business website's checkout page.

For disconnected shops, you can look over Bitcoin terminals or Point-Of-Sale applications, for example, XBTerminal, Coinify or Coingate. You can likewise print out QR

codes that your clients can examine with their portable wallets and effectively pay you in bitcoins.

Once your bitcoin wallet is set up, you should simply report to the entire world you're prepared to acknowledge Bitcoin installments!

The Most Effective Method To Handle The Volatility Of Bitcoin

The prospect of losing your benefits and basically giving without end your stock for nothing to your clients is one frightening idea as you can rapidly go bankrupt if every one of your clients paid in bitcoin.

At a certain point in time it might have been valid, however with Bitcoin installment processors like Coinbase and BitPay, it's currently conceivable to get your installments in bitcoin and have it immediately changed over to US dollars or some other bolstered cash. Thusly you keep away from every one of the dangers related with bitcoin and get the full dollar sum you should get.

To delineate, if your client pays you $100 worth of bitcoin for a couple of pants, at that point you will get precisely $100 in your ledger. The installment passage you use, for instance BitPay, will shield you from bitcoin's unpredictability so you generally get the full dollar sum.

For the additionally ambitious entrepreneurs who can deal with Bitcoin's unconventionality, the chance to make significantly more benefit from the bitcoins they've been paid with may be overpowering.

On the off chance that you have a place with this class, you would most likely keep your bitcoins in your computerized wallets, and forego the utilization of an installment processor who will naturally change over your bitcoins to dollars.

Why Your Business Should Start Accepting Bitcoin Payments

Bitcoin was made by Satoshi Nakamoto because of the 2008 money related market crash which relatively injured the whole worldwide economy. He made it to take care of or beat the issues we have with having a concentrated keeping money framework that profited banks more than they did shoppers.

Simply consider the bank charges you need to pay everytime somebody pays you for your item or administration. Store charges, withdrawal expenses, exchange expenses, Visa expenses, and a wide range of expenses are deducted from your well deserved cash.

Bitcoin's motivation was to keep away from all that, and this distributed electronic money framework was Satoshi Nakamoto's answer for the issue. The framework was made basically so everybody gets what is expected them without the pointless mediation of banks and government.

The Benefits Of Bitcoin Payments For Your Business

There are a lot of advantages for your business in the event that you begin tolerating bitcoin installments. Here are some of them:

No Risk Of Chargebacks

Paypal, credit and check card installments depart your business helpless against chargebacks. Most, if not all, organizations (both on the web and disconnected traders) have likely encountered this issue at some point. Managing a chargeback is a cerebral pain initiating and tedious process.

Your clients can claim to not perceive the charge on their card explanations, or their card was stolen and another person utilized it to purchase from you, or they're disturbed that your stock was not as depicted or it was imperfect.

A few people essentially get a kick out of the chance to do chargebacks on the grounds that they need to get a thing for nothing, particularly if it's a high-esteem thing. Obviously, this is an exceptionally untrustworthy activity, however you can't foresee your clients' practices.

With Bitcoin installments, there is zero danger of chargebacks in light of the fact that all installments, once it has been affirmed, are last. There is no chance to get for anybody, not even the savviest and sharpest software engineers on the planet, can turn around or fix a bitcoin exchange.

Bitcoin installments offer trader assurance that is unparalleled by some other installment alternative accessible today. No bank and no administration can give you the level of vendor assurance that Bitcoin does.

No Fraud And Double Payments

The Bitcoin arrange is a greatly secure installment framework. Not at all like banks, Bitcoin is upright. Before Bitcoin went along, twofold installments and extortion were an undeniable issue with advanced money however fortunately, on account of the endeavors of Satoshi Nakamoto, the issue of twofold spending was at long last explained.

Bitcoin is a decentralized, shared installment framework. Everybody on the system sees all the bitcoin exchanges that have ever occurred. This straightforwardness makes it troublesome for fraudsters to counterfeit records so they can spend a similar measure of bitcoins twice or twofold spend it.

This gigantic record, otherwise called the blockchain, keeps a record of all exchanges. An exchange is just added to a square once it has been affirmed or checked by diggers that the exchange is substantial.

Close Instant Payments

Bitcoin installments are quick, unalterable and last. There's no chance to get for anybody to fix any bitcoin exchange. As long you show the right bitcoin deliver for your clients to pay into, you're ready, and your bitcoins will touch base in your wallet more often than not inside 10-45 minutes.

Utilizing the right bitcoin address is clearly an imperative point to consider in light of the fact that if by any shot, you exhibit the wrong bitcoin address, at that point there's no chance to get for you to recuperate those bitcoins. Unless obviously, you know who claims that bitcoin address, at that point you can basically request that they send those bitcoins to your right address.

Another upside to utilizing installment doors like Coinbase and BitPay is that you can get your trade out your financial balances inside 2-3 days. These administrations more often than not send installments each business day (not everytime an exchange happens).

On the other hand, in the event that you need to keep your bitcoins, that is, you would prefer not to change over them to dollars, at that point that is flawlessly fine. You can choose this alternative in your installment passage settings. In any case, you will get your bitcoins or your dollars helpfully and in less time than if the client paid with Paypal or a Mastercard.

Unimportant Transaction Fees

With bitcoin installments, you get the chance to keep a greater amount of what your client pays you. You viably cut out the broker (your bank) with their costly charges. You will in any case need to pay a little bitcoin exchange expense which goes to the excavators who confirm all bitcoin exchanges and add it to the record or blockchain.

This exchange charge is relatively irrelevant and is a unimportant equal to pennies, not at all like the expenses your bank or Visa organization expects you to pay!

For Visa installments, vendors are typically charged a trade expense (paid to the bank or card backer) and an appraisal expense (paid to the Mastercard organization, for example, Visa or Mastercard). By and large, these expenses will wind up costing the trader around 3% to 4% for every exchange.

In correlation, for bitcoin exchanges, the expenses are commonly around 10,000 Satoshis or 0.0001 bitcoin. You're allowed to set your own charges, yet the higher the exchange expense you set per exchange, the speedier bitcoin mineworkers will affirm your exchange.

For a $1,000 charge card installment, the expenses that shippers need to pay would be around $30 to $40. For a comparable buy sum paid for in bitcoin, the exchange charge would generally be around $1 if the current bitcoin cost is say, for instance, $10,000 per bitcoin ($10,000 x 0.0001 = $1).

You would already be able to see just by this illustration that bitcoin exchanges will spare you a considerable measure of cash just in exchange charges. Envision the amount you will get the chance to spare in case you're ready to offer your $1,000 item only 10 times each day or 100 times each day!

Expanded Sales And More Profit For You

Bitcoin doesn't separate where anybody originates from. Regardless of whether your client lives in a nation known for charge card misrepresentation, in Bitcoin's eyes everybody is equivalent. On the off chance that you've at any point endeavored to acknowledge installments from clients in these nations, you know exactly how troublesome and awkward the whole procedure is.

Paypal, Stripe and other well known installment passages don't acknowledge or bolster numerous nations with high pervasiveness of misrepresentation. However, with Bitcoin, you can without much of a stretch acknowledge installments from any individual who lives anyplace on the planet. All they have to pay you is only your bitcoin address!

They don't have to send their photographs and national ID cards, so your clients' security is all around ensured. Furthermore, as you definitely know, all bitcoin exchanges are last, so there's no chance to get for any of your clients to complete a chargeback like they effectively can with a Visa.

Bitcoin makes the world a littler and better place. It deletes outskirts, government formality, and administration. It permits dealers and entrepreneurs like you to get installments from clients who are sufficiently terrible to live in nations with a high extortion rate.

Bitcoin ensures you and your business. In the meantime, it enables you to give your administration and your items to everybody in the entire world.

More Joyful Customers

Adding Bitcoin to your rundown of bolstered installments will give your clients an additional decision to hand over their cash to you. Regardless of whether they don't have bitcoins yet, they may in the end get into the amusement at some point or another.

Also, when they do, they'll recall you and prescribe you to their companions. Notwithstanding existing clients will be cheerful to know you've included Bitcoin installments.

In case you're one of only a handful couple of organizations in your group that acknowledges Bitcoin installments, at that point you're most likely going to end up noticeably prominent in light of the fact that you'll be seen as an imaginative and ground breaking business.

Many individuals have found out about Bitcoin on the news, and many would have built up a passing interest or have started to end up plainly inquisitive about bitcoins and digital money when all is said in done. You can instruct your clients and let them recognize what Bitcoin is and how it will help them in their money related exchanges.

Consider it, would you rather be one of the primary organizations to offer Bitcoin installments and take your rival's clients all the while? Or on the other hand would you rather have your clients go to your opposition essentially on the grounds that they offer Bitcoin installments, and you don't?

Get Support From The Bitcoin Community

The Bitcoin people group is developing quick, and with soaring bitcoin costs, they are searching for places where they can spend their bitcoins. Various enormous organizations have added Bitcoin to their installment alternatives, yet an extraordinary

larger part of organizations still can't seem to stick to this same pattern. So when the Bitcoin people group finds another business that backings bitcoin, they share the news with everybody. That is free commercial for your business, and you can anticipate that them will drop by your site or physical store at any point in the near future.

To get adequate presentation to the Bitcoin people group, you can spread the news via web-based networking media, in Bitcoin gatherings, pages, gatherings, and so on. In the event that you have a physical store, you should likewise put a substantial billboard outside that will report to anybody going by that you're tolerating Bitcoin installments.

Developing your business doesn't need to be troublesome. Tolerating Bitcoin installments won't just make your business famous among the Bitcoin people group, yet it will likewise prompt more deals and more benefits for you.

Chapter 7: Step by Step instructions to Protect Yourself Against Fraud And Theft

Bitcoin and cryptographic forms of money are hot wares at this moment. Everybody needs a slice of the profits, however with taking off costs, many can't stand to purchase and contribute out of their own pockets.

So they do the following best thing they can consider – trick and take these valuable advanced coins from other individuals. In this guide, we'll demonstrate to you probably the most widely recognized tricks these extortionists are running and additionally how you can ensure yourself against them.

Bitcoin And Cryptocurrencies Are Not Scams

Before we go into the primary tricks you ought to know about, we'd get a kick out of the chance to bring up that these tricks are all from outside powers, and not digital forms of money themselves. You may hear a few people say that cryptographic forms of money are only an enormous trick yet it's 100% false, and we'll clarify why.

The innovation behind digital forms of money is known as the blockchain. It is a morally sound advanced record that records all exchanges in the system. No focal body controls it. It is straightforward, and anybody can track any exchange that has ever occurred before.

Nobody can adjust any exchange recorded on the blockchain in light of the fact that doing as such would mean you'd need to change whatever is left of the exchanges or obstructs that came after that specific exchange; this is for all intents and purposes an incomprehensible errand to do.

The blockchain is secure to the point that many banks and new businesses are currently testing, and beginning to execute blockchain innovation since they've seen exactly how well it deals with Bitcoin and digital forms of money.

Since you know you can put stock in the innovation behind digital forms of money, we should talk about the most widely recognized tricks that many individuals fall prey to.

Trick #1 – Fake Bitcoin Exchanges

There are a lot of respectable bitcoin trades today. The greatest and most prevalent stages that have been around a couple of years are Coinbase, Kraken, CEX.io, Changelly, Bitstamp, Poloniex, and Bitfinex. All things considered, we can't vouch for any organization regardless of whether they're notable in the business.

You should do your due persistence by inquiring about the organization's history, client surveys, and decide for yourself whether you need to spend your well deserved fiat cash with them.

Pipe dream Exchange Rates

Because of the very unpredictable nature of digital forms of money (costs can go here and there by a gigantic spread in only a couple of hours!), numerous unpalatable characters on the Internet are profiting by this instability. They go after clueless tenderfoots who can't detect the distinction between a honest to goodness trade and a phony one.

These phony bitcoin trades can without much of a stretch set up decent looking sites and awe individuals with their apparently modern look. They snare individuals

in with their guarantees of lower-than-showcase rate costs and ensured returns. Basically, they play on individuals' avarice.

Envision how elate you'd learn about in the event that you found about a site that offers bitcoins at 10% or 20% lower rates than the going rates on Coinbase or Kraken. In the event that these expansive stages are putting forth $15,000 for 1 bitcoin, and this other site is putting forth it at $12,000, wouldn't you seize the possibility?

You'd spare so much ($3,000 per bitcoin!), and you can utilize your investment funds to purchase significantly more bitcoins. It couldn't be any more obvious, that is them playing on ravenousness! They realize that individuals need to purchase more bitcoins for less dollars. Also, who can accuse those poor casualties? In the event that we didn't know any better, we may fall for a similar trick as well.

Get Instant PayPal Payment For Your Bitcoins

Another strategy these phony bitcoin trades use to take your bitcoins is they'll offer to purchase your coins at higher-than-advertise rates, and after that send the comparable dollar add up to your PayPal address.

To the clueless bitcoin proprietor, he supposes he's showing signs of improvement end of the arrangement since he will get more cash for his bitcoins, and he'll get the trade in a flash out his PayPal account.

In this way, he enters the measure of bitcoins he needs to offer, affirms he's content with the comparable dollar sum, types in his PayPal address so they can send the cash to him, at that point he pauses. What's more, pauses. What's more, holds up some more.

He'll contact the site at the same time, obviously, they're not going to answer to him now since they have his bitcoins (recollect, all bitcoin exchanges are last and irreversible once approved).

Now, he'll understand he's simply been misled. He can report the site and compose awful audits, however who's he joking? These canny con artists will simply set up shop under another space name and sit tight for their next casualty.

The key takeaway here is to avoid 'trades' with pipe dream rates. As the colloquialism goes, if it's unrealistic, it most likely is.

Trick #2 – Phishing Scams

There are such a large number of sorts of phishing tricks that run uncontrolled today. Ever gotten an email from your 'bank' asking you check or refresh your record points of interest to ensure your subtle elements stay exceptional? Furthermore, that you need to tap on the email connect to refresh your points of interest?

Many individuals know these sorts of messages are just a trick. Current email administrations send these garbage messages to the garbage organizer at any rate, so you don't see them all that much these days.

Be that as it may, with Bitcoin and cryptographic money being so new thus hot in the news at this moment, tricksters are scrambling to figure out how to take your bitcoins by accessing your advanced wallets!

Email Phishing Scams

Con artists will send you an email intended to influence it to seem as though it originated from your online wallet benefit (this is the reason we don't recommend putting away huge aggregates of virtual money in your trade wallets).

In the email, they'll request that you tap on a connection which will lead you to a phony site. It will look precisely like your trade or wallet site. Obviously, it's not the same on the grounds that the space name will be unique.

For instance, in case you're utilizing Coinbase, they'll utilize a comparative incorrectly spelled area, for example,

• Cooinbase

• Coiinbase

• Coinbasse

• Coinsbase

• Coinbase-Client-Update.com

• or something comparative...

It will likewise most presumably not have a security include called SSL introduced, which implies the space will begin with HTTP and not HTTPS (present day programs like Chrome and Firefox ought to caution you if it's a safe site or not).

On the off chance that you succumb to this phishing trick, and you sign in to the phony wallet site, at that point the con artists now have your login subtle elements to your genuine wallet! They can undoubtedly keep you out of your record, and they'll at that point have the opportunity to exchange each and every bitcoin you possess to their own wallets.

Malware Scams

In this sort of trick, con artists will request that you tap on a connection either through email, pennant advertisement, gathering promotion, or anyplace they can post a connection which will then download a kind of malware to your PC.

Frequently, these malwares are keyloggers which will record all that you compose on your PC, and send the data to the tricksters. In this way, in the event that you sign in to your online wallet, as Coinbase for instance, they will have the capacity to see your username and your secret word, and they would then be able to sign in to your record and effortlessly take your coins from you!

The key takeaway for shielding yourself from these sorts of tricks is to never tap on joins from dishonest sources.

In the event that you don't perceive the sender, or the site space name is incorrectly spelled, it should raise a warning, and you should report the email as well as leave the phishing site immediately.

Besides, consider utilizing disconnected putting away strategies, for example, paper wallets or equipment wallets so regardless of whether con artists access your online wallet, they'll have nothing to take there.

Trick #3 – Cloud Mining Scams

Cloud mining is a prevalent method for turning into a bitcoin mineworker. You never again need to put resources into your own particular supercomputer and join a mining gathering to tackle complex cryptographic hash issues. You don't have to stress over costly power bills.

You essentially need to join to a cloud mining administration (otherwise called a mining ranch), lease mining hardware, and get installments proportionate to your membership.

While some cloud mining organizations are true blue, there are many here now gone again later sites which guarantee implausible returns for measly wholes, whose sole reason for existing is to take your cash.

Some basic warnings to keep an eye out for when hoping to join a cloud mining administration is the nonattendance of an About page, Terms of Use/Service page, physical address, and additionally contact number.

They may likewise not have a protected area (no HTTPS previously their space name). These subtle elements are altogether critical in making sense of which site is a trick and which isn't. You can look Google for audits and experience their site to get a vibe on the off chance that they're true blue or not. As a general rule, these destinations would be mysterious without any names or faces behind them.

Some may seem real at first however investigate what your venture will get you. You may pay in the long run agree to accept an agreement which will cost you a couple of thousand dollars every year except what are you going to receive consequently? You'll need to figure it out yourself and compute in case you will wind up in the green.

The key takeaway here is before you spend any of your well deserved fiat cash, you ought to at any rate ensure you're managing a honest to goodness organization and not some unknown con artist who'll abandon you in tears.

Do a lot of research, read surveys, and peruse the crypto-digging groups for data on the best and most reliable cloud mining organizations.

Trick #4 – Ponzi Scams

Ponzi tricks are likely less demanding to spot than alternate tricks we've shrouded so far in this guide. This is on the grounds that Ponzi tricks are outstanding for ensuring extraordinary profits for ventures with practically zero hazard to the financial specialists. Individuals fall for these sorts of tricks all the time since individuals need ensured returns on their speculations.

With Bitcoin and digital currency, any organization that ensures exponential profits for any speculation ought to be seen as a potential con artist. The digital money showcase is exceedingly unstable, and one moment the cost could be at an unsurpassed high and the following, it's around a couple of hundred or a couple of thousand dollars.

In light of this unpredictability, you ought to never trust any individual who reveals to you you're ensured a 10% profit for your venture each and every day, or whatever the con artist's terms might be.

Since Ponzi plans depend on new individuals, a.k.a. casualties, to pay off their initial speculators, they typically offer motivations for individuals to select new individuals to join their system.

It's exceptionally regular for tricks like this to offer some type of member rewards. You allude somebody to put resources into the 'organization,' and you get made up for your endeavors.

Some Ponzi plans ensure day by day benefits until the end of time. On the off chance that this appears to be inconceivable, it assuredly is. Nobody even knows whether bitcoins will associate with that long and ensuring every day returns is simply insane. Immediately, a smart financial specialist will see that offers like these are simply tricks intended to scam you your cash or your bitcoins.

Indeed, a large number of these trick locales lean toward bitcoin installments since they know Bitcoin exchanges can't be turned around or drop once sent! In any case, regardless of whether they require fiat or cryptographic money, know who you're sending your cash to first.

The key takeaway here is whether you know the organization's offers are unrealistic, at that point you should flee the other way. Some of the time, there's simply no reason for looking into audits on the

Internet with regards to tricks like these on the grounds that most 'commentators' are the individuals who got in the diversion early and in this manner have officially gotten some arrival on their speculation.

What's more, generally, when these clients leave surveys they'll incorporate their partner connect so you know immediately they have a personal stake for leaving gleaming audits for an organization they may, or may not know, is a trick.

Chapter 8: The Future Of Cryptocurrency

Before we discuss the fate of digital currency, it's imperative to help ourselves to remember the past and what cryptographic money resembled in the first place. In 2008, when Bitcoin originator, Satoshi Nakamoto, first discharged his whitepaper on Bitcoin, many individuals said it was only a prevailing fashion and a trick intended to trap individuals into surrendering their 'genuine' cash.

There were numerous naysayers and monetary specialists who said Bitcoin will never be received by the majority and will fail and cease to exist in a year or something like that.

Luckily, the cryptographic money group encouraged and cooperated to make Bitcoin a win. They saw potential in the blockchain innovation and what it could mean for the fund division. They saw the requirement for cryptographic money in light of the fact that the current budgetary setup through banks and governments had an excessive number of issues and was making national economies crumple.

They saw that keeping expansion under control was troublesome with conventional monetary forms and the poorest individuals frequently have no simple access to banks. Accepting or sending installments was customarily a cerebral pain with exchange charges gobbling up a lot of cash.

Banks charge extravagant expenses just so their clients can access their own one of a kind cash, and the administration makes next to no move, if by any stretch of the imagination, to help the general population.

Bitcoin supporters say the advanced budgetary framework is where banks and governments connive or cooperate, not to help their nationals'

budgetary requirements, however to take as much cash as they can from them regarding charges gathered.

Bitcoin changed all that. With Bitcoin, you're removing the agent. There are no more banks to manage and no legislature to keep an eye on your ledgers. With Bitcoin, you are your own bank. You're the bank employee sending and accepting installments, and you're the investor accountable for guarding your cash.

Bitcoin has been a pioneer on such a large number of fronts. As the principal effective digital money, it has made ready for different cryptographic forms of money to succeed and the worldwide group has gradually paid heed these previous couple of years. Read on to discover what different conceivable outcomes Bitcoin and cryptographic forms of money bring for what's to come!

In most created nations, getting a charge card or a business advance is moderately simple. Be that as it may, in creating nations, you'd need to actually go through the motions and government formality before you can get one. However, with Bitcoin and cryptographic money, all you require is only your computerized wallet, and you can begin accepting digital currency from anybody, anyplace on the planet.

You don't require your own Internet association at home; you can basically run some place with great Internet get to and make a speedy wallet on the web or on your cell phone. Obviously, putting away your crypto online isn't a smart thought so you should investigate putting away these in icy stockpiling, for example, an equipment wallet or paper wallet.

In any case, online wallets are incredible for little exchanges so in the event that you have to pay a service charge or your Mastercard charge, essentially check the service organization's bitcoin wallet's QR code and send your crypto installment. No compelling reason to spend the entire day remaining in long queues!

Today, there are as of now numerous organizations which have begun to acknowledge bitcoin installments (however they are still in the minority). These ground breaking entrepreneurs see the advantage of tolerating bitcoins and are benefitting pleasantly from this savvy business choice!

You can purchase for all intents and purposes anything with bitcoins. You can purchase plane tickets, you can lease autos, you can pay for your school educational cost, you can purchase basic needs, you can purchase stuff on Amazon by buying Amazon gift vouchers on outsider locales, thus substantially more!

Later on, we can expect such a large number of more organizations to hop onto the bitcoin installment wagon, and it would be a win-win circumstance for both entrepreneurs and clients.

Organizations will get their installment quick and into their ledgers the precise following day (utilizing an installment door like BitPay which offers moment bitcoins to fiat cash transformation), and clients will get the chance to purchase things in an extremely advantageous way.

Bitcoin In Developing Economies

It's not astounding that Bitcoin has seen monstrous selection as of late. Truth be told, in Zimbabwe, individuals are utilizing bitcoins to make monetary exchanges. With the end of the Zimbabwean dollar, the nation needed to fall back on utilizing US dollars as their principle cash.

Be that as it may, this isn't an extremely doable arrangement in light of the fact that their administration can't print US dollars themselves. Venezuelans are additionally encountering a similar issue. The Venezuelan bolivar has moved toward becoming so hyper-expanded it's relatively unusable. Individuals have turned to utilizing bitcoins to pay for essential merchandise, prescriptions, goods, thus considerably more.

For the Zimbabweans and Venezuelans, and in addition the Vietnamese, Colombians, and nationals of nations with super swelled monetary forms, Bitcoin is a reference point of light since it's not subject to the impulses and controls of their nearby banks or their legislatures.

Their present monetary circumstance is an ideal case of the drawback of having a focal expert to deal with a nation's money, while in the meantime, it features every one of the advantages of utilizing Bitcoin, a decentralized and 100% straightforward budgetary system.

With Bitcoin getting huge help from individuals in creating nations, governments may soon be venturing in to direct the utilization of Bitcoin and different digital currencies. While we can't foresee the future, for the present, Bitcoin gives a superb expansion less other option to conventional cash.

What's more, with soaring Bitcoin and cryptographic money costs, this gives many individuals a great deal of obtaining influence which their national monetary forms can't give.

Quick And Cheap International Payments

One of the fundamental advantages of bitcoin installments is the speed by which the beneficiary can get their bitcoins. This is ideal for individuals who enlist consultants or workers abroad.

The representatives don't have to agree to accept a financial balance and acquire charges left and right since they're getting cash from yourself, a global customer.

Obviously, we should not neglect to say the expenses that you yourself will pay to your bank everytime you dispatch or exchange monies to your abroad laborers.

Notwithstanding the charges both you and your beneficiary pay, you'd likewise need to factor in the conversion standard. Most banks and cash exchange administrations will as a rule let you know in advance that "this" is the present swapping scale yet when you contrast it with genuine rates, the bank rate would be much lower.

Notwithstanding for PayPal installments, you'll see a distinction in the conversion standard they utilize. You presumably won't see the conversion scale when you're exchanging generally little sums, yet when you're executing in a large number of dollars, the expenses can rapidly indicate a noteworthy sum.

With Bitcoin, you can state farewell to all these over the top charges.

For each bitcoin exchange, you do need to pay a little expense for the excavators, however it's truly nothing contrasted with what your banks are charging you! Regardless of whether you're sending 1,000 bitcoins or 0.01 bitcoins, the mining expense can be the same since the charge is figured as far as bytes, not the measure of bitcoins.

The size (in bytes) of your exchange will rely upon the quantity of sources of info and yields per exchange. Without delving into the specialized points of interest, what's vital to observe here is the mining charges are, little

contrasted with your bank's expenses. This is the reason Bitcoin and digital money will change what's to come. More individuals will execute with each other straightforwardly to abstain from paying those exceptionally costly bank expenses!

With an ever increasing number of individuals sending cryptographic money to each other straightforwardly, there might be no more requirement for outsider cash exchange benefits or even banks. In spite of the fact that this may take numerous years to happen, it's as yet a plausibility once everybody gets instructed on the advantages of utilizing cryptographic money to send and get installments from anybody on the planet in only a couple of minutes.

Battle Crime and Corruption

Many individuals are stressed that the Bitcoin arrange is being utilized by tax criminals, lawbreakers, and degenerate authorities since they believe it's a mysterious system. Indeed, all checked exchanges are recorded on the blockchain and no, there are no names recorded there.

You can see just alphanumeric codes, loads of it truth be told. On the off chance that you download the free and open source Bitcoin Core customer, you'll likewise need to download the whole blockchain which is as of now more than 100GB+. A large number of bitcoin exchanges since 2009 are put away on the blockchain. You'll even observe the main ever exchange by its organizer, Satoshi Nakamoto.

We're specifying this to point to the way that Bitcoin isn't generally unknown. Rather, it's pseudonymous, which means clients can hole up behind aliases, on close investigation, advanced legal sciences specialists can follow who claims Bitcoin wallets.

This is, obviously, a tedious undertaking yet when you're after lawbreakers who've washed millions or billions of dollars of bitcoins at that point getting them turns into a best need. Truth be told, specialists say that culprits are in an ideal situation reserving their stolen plunder in seaward ledgers with their super strict bank protection laws.

Be that as it may, bitcoin is simpler to move around so individuals figure they can without much of a stretch shroud their illegal exchanges in the alphanumeric labyrinth known as the blockchain. To put it plainly, various lawbreakers have been put in the slammer on account of Bitcoin and the blockchain.

Later on, if and when cryptographic money increases gigantic help and appropriation from the majority around the world, it will be less demanding for specialists to follow and get culprits planning to utilize digital currencies as a way to stow away and move their stolen cash around.

Blockchain Technology Will Become Mainstream

Numerous administrations, banks, and private associations are investigating receiving the blockchain innovation into their items and administrations. The blockchain is the fundamental innovation behind Bitcoin and different cryptographic forms of money.

The innovation is as of now accepting acknowledgment and reception from numerous parts on the planet. While this may take quite a long while, it's no less than a positive gesture for the blockchain upset.

Two of the most well known blockchain innovations today are Ethereum and Hyperledger. You may have known about Ethereum as the second most prevalent cryptographic money, after Bitcoin. Be that as it may, it's something beyond a virtual cash stage.

Ethereum is a stage that enables anybody to make shrewd contracts which enable individuals to exchange or trade anything of significant worth, for example, cash, property, stocks, and so on. The agreement is openly straightforward and is recorded on the blockchain which implies other individuals are observer to the assention.

The best thing about keen contracts is you are essentially computerizing contracts without paying for the administrations of a go between, for example, a bank, stockbroker, or legal counselor.

Hyperledger, then again, is an open source, cross-industry collective venture with donors from many real organizations, for example, Deutsche Bank, IBM, Airbus and SAP.

As indicated by their site, the joint effort means to build up "another age of value-based applications that set up confide in, responsibility and straightforwardness." These applications can possibly streamline business forms and lessen the cost and multifaceted nature of different frameworks in reality.

These are only a couple of cases of how blockchain innovation will change the world later on. Blockchain might be not as much as 10 years old, however it has effectively changed the lives of such a significant number of individuals to improve things.

In this guide, you've adapted such a large number of advantages of utilizing Bitcoin, digital money and blockchain innovation. Putting resources into cryptographic money might be to your greatest advantage however it's constantly best to do top to bottom research on which digital money to put resources into.

Bitcoin might be excessively costly until further notice however recall that you don't need to purchase an entire bitcoin. Then again, there are other developing cryptographic forms of money with great track records you may consider putting resources into.

With digital currency looking set to get incorporated with standard money related markets, putting resources into cryptographic money isn't a startling idea any longer. Indeed, it could conceivably be the best money related choice you'll ever make for yourself and your family's future.

Thanks again for buying my book. If you have a minute, please leave a positive review. You can leave your review by clicking on this link:

Leave your review here. Thank you!

I take reviews seriously and always look at them. This way, you are helping me provide you better content that you will LOVE in the future. A review doesn't have to be long, just one or two sentences and a number of stars you find appropriate (hopefully 5 of course).

Also, if I think your review is useful, I will mark it as "helpful." This will help you become more known on Amazon as a decent reviewer, and will ensure that more authors will contact you with free e-books in the future. This is how we can help each other.

www.ingramcontent.com/pod-product-compliance
Lightning Source LLC
Chambersburg PA
CBHW071321220526
45468CB00001B/455